D0387115

ECONOMICS

What Went Wrong, and Why,
and Some Things to Do About It

ECONOMICS

WHAT WENT WRONG, AND WHY, AND SOME THINGS TO DO ABOUT IT

GEORGE P. BROCKWAY

A Cornelia & Michael Bessie Book

HARPER & ROW, PUBLISHERS, New York
*Cambridge, Philadelphia, San Francisco, London
Mexico City, São Paulo, Singapore, Sydney*

Portions of this book have appeared, in somewhat different form, in *The New Leader*, *Washington Monthly*, and *Journal of Post Keynesian Economics*.

ECONOMICS: WHAT WENT WRONG, AND WHY, AND SOME THINGS TO DO ABOUT IT. Copyright © 1985 by George P. Brockway. All rights reserved. Printed in the United States of America. No part of this book may be used or reproduced in any manner whatsoever without written permission except in the case of brief quotations embodied in critical articles and reviews. For information address Harper & Row, Publishers, Inc., 10 East 53rd Street, New York, N.Y. 10022. Published simultaneously in Canada by Fitzhenry & Whiteside Limited, Toronto.

FIRST EDITION

Designer: Sidney Feinberg

This book is set in 11-point Caledonia. It was composed by Fisher Composition, Inc., New York, N.Y., and printed and bound by R. R. Donnelley and Sons Company, the Lakeside Press, Chicago.

Library of Congress Cataloging in Publication Data

Brockway, George P.
    Economics: what went wrong, and why, and some things
to do about it.

    "Portions of this book have appeared . . . in the
New leader, Washington monthly, and Journal of post
Keynesian economics"—T.p. verso.
    "A Cornelia & Michael Bessie book."
    Includes index.
    1. Economics. I. Title.
HB171.B6498 1985   330   84-47559
ISBN 0-06-039037-9

85 86 87 88 89 10 9 8 7 6 5 4 3 2 1

LIBRARY
The University of Texas
At San Antonio

To the memory of

JOHN WILLIAM MILLER

CONTENTS

PREFACE

The great Confucius said that he would rather be
a profound political economist than chief of police.
—MARK TWAIN, *Sketches Old and New*

In the famous peroration of *The General Theory of Employment, Interest and Money,* John Maynard Keynes wrote that "Practical men, who believe themselves to be quite exempt from any intellectual influences, are usually the slaves of some defunct economist." In the same way, living economists, who believe themselves to be quite exempt from what they may think of as academic logic-chopping, are usually the slaves of some defunct philosopher. The first four chapters of this book are therefore devoted to uncovering certain assumptions that are silently, and often unconsciously, made by many economists and, through them, by many statesmen, businessmen, and citizens generally. That these assumptions are not ordinarily discussed by economists, or even noticed, is responsible for much of the confusion that surrounds the subject and contributes to the grievous derangement of public policy.

The next eight chapters build on the first four and touch, in possibly unfamiliar ways, on familiar topics in economic theory. Questions of public policy inevitably intrude in these middle chapters, and such questions provide the subject matter of the penultimate three, whose purpose is not to exhaust any subject, much less the range of subjects, but to illustrate the principles developed in the earlier chapters.

The book is in one sense a call to action; but more fundamentally, it is a call to understanding.

Thinking about basic questions cannot be effortless, but at least it can avoid being deliberately murky; therefore I have tried to make the most of ordinary speech. Even for professionals, jargon can be a barrier to, and sometimes a substitute for, thought. A few terms, nevertheless, are defined with some care and are used in a somewhat unusual way. The most important of these are *profit, speculation,* and *investment*; and the most important formulation based on them is what I call the Labor Theory of Right.

There is no idea presented here that is not directly or indirectly due to the teaching of the late Professor John William Miller of Williams College. Even turns of phrase and sentence rhythms are often his, as readers of the five volumes of his published essays will recognize. In addition, much of the material covered here was discussed with him in person or by correspondence. I make no claim that he would have supported what I have written, but my indebtedness to him is beyond possibility of repayment.

I am also indebted to Myron Kolatch, executive editor of *The New Leader,* who has, for several years now, provided me with a bully pulpit for trying out my ideas. Of several professional economists who have helped me, the first in every way was the late Professor Sidney Weintraub of the University of Pennsylvania, a man of incisive mind, encyclopedic interests, boundless enthusiasm, and infinite generosity. Professor Paul Davidson of Rutgers, formerly co-editor with Professor Weintraub of the *Journal of Post Keynesian Economics* and now sole editor, read the entire manuscript, helped me in clarifying many points, and saved me from many errors. Professor Thomas Mayer of the University of California, Davis, generously made useful comments on Chapter 15 even though he disagreed with much of it.

Others who have read some or all of the manuscript include my friends (and fellow students of Professor Miller's) Philip A. Brégy and Professor Robert H. Elias; my business colleagues Eric P. Swenson (who pushed me into writing economics), William H. Onysko, John E. Neill, Donald S. Lamm, Victor Schmalzer, and Edwin Barber; my ally in forgotten political battles, Norman Jacobs; Simon Michael Bessie, my long-time friend and now my editor, whose faith and support made it possible for me to write; my wife, Lucile, whose insights, enriched by anthropological studies, have humanized many otherwise abstract problems in this book and in our life; and our children.

All of these good people made helpful suggestions, most of which I have had the wit to adopt. I am grateful to them all, and of course absolve them of all responsibility for the errors and weaknesses that remain.

Practically all of the statistics herein come from the 1984 "Economic Report of the President." I have omitted bibliographical references, though the book is liberally salted with quotations, because it seems to me that the book stands or falls on its ideas, not its scholarship. The index was prepared by Sydney Wolfe Cohen.

—GEORGE P. BROCKWAY

ECONOMICS

What Went Wrong, and Why,
and Some Things to Do About It

1

BACKGROUND

Glimpses of the World Before and After Adam Smith

i

We will define economics as the study of the principles whereby people exchange money for goods and services. Of the words in our definition, "people" is obviously the most important, though it tends to become blurred or to drop out of sight altogether in almost all contemporary discussion of the subject. Because we will keep people steadily in view, we will see economics as a humanistic discipline. Because it is humanistic, it is normative; that is, it proposes standards of right action. Because there are no absolute standards, it is historical. While the words in standard definitions of the discipline may not differ markedly from those we have used, the emphasis is entirely different. As we have said, "people" is the most important word in our definition; but Adam Smith took the wealth of nations for his subject, and modern schools concentrate on the gross national product.

At this point we can give only a bare suggestion of how this difference of emphasis works. In the early 1980s, when upwards of fourteen million men and women in the United States were unemployed, and there was much debate about whether we were in a recession or a depression, and how to end whatever it was, public attention was lavished on statistics supposed to indicate when recovery was finally under way. Among the "indicators," the rate of unemployment was

1

understandably included. But this rate was, curiously, a "lagging" indicator. That is to say, standard economics held that something entitled to be called a recovery could be achieved leaving 6 or 8 or even 10 percent of our fellow citizens unemployed.

An economics that is thus willing to disregard several million people will clearly differ in substantial ways from an economics that holds that full and just employment of men and women is the economic problem, and that a business recovery *may* be a means to that end, but certainly is not an end in itself.

ii

It is a journalistic commonplace that all modern schools of economics, from far left to far right, are in disarray. If this is so, it is because the foundations of the discipline, which were laid in 1776 by Adam Smith, are now crumbling. These foundations were built on by Karl Marx no less than by John Stuart Mill. It has taken two hundred years for cracks in the foundations to become suspected, and it will undoubtedly take a while longer before the suspected cracks are seen, and even longer before it is recognized that they are beyond repair. In the meantime we shall all suffer from recurrent symptoms of unemployment, inflation, and international disorder, while confused teams of economists, businessmen, bankers, and statesmen search despairingly for a cure.

Adam Smith was certainly not an isolated figure in the history of thought; and we will better understand both his achievement and its limitations if we make at least a provisional attempt to place him in his time. The great movement of which he was a part, and of which we may now be seeing the end, made its first stirrings in the natural sciences. Copernicus may conveniently be considered the beginning, though of course many were those who were before him. His dates (1473–1543) roughly coincide with or overlap Piero della Francesca's *Resurrection* and Michelangelo's *Last*

Judgment, Columbus's discovery of America, Luther's post-ing of the ninety-five theses on the door of the Saxony castle church, and the consolidation of nation states in France un-der Louis XI and Charles VIII and in England under the Tudors. It was a turbulent time, the death of an old world.

Copernicus's contribution was an early glimpse of a ra-tional and impersonal natural world. What he did was only slowly appreciated. It is possible that he himself had an ink-ling of the dangers inherent in his book on the revolutions of the heavenly bodies, for it was not published until he lay on his deathbed, though he had evidently finished it thirteen years previously. Nevertheless, the book circulated quietly for almost a hundred years before the Church prosecuted Galileo for expounding its ideas. Today it is often protested that there is no conflict between science and religion, and that the prosecution of Galileo was unnecessary and a strate-gic mistake. This is an anachronism. The Church was surely prescient in fearing the consequences of a heliocentric uni-verse, and the professors at Padua had good reason to be wary of what they might see if they looked through Galileo's telescope. There was no longer an actual place for Heaven above or for Hell below. In simplifying the harmony of the spheres, Copernicus had put the whole medieval synthesis at risk.

The threat to the Church lay less in the discovery of new facts about the world, startling though they were, than in the development of a new way of thinking about the world. Galileo was not the first to demonstrate that Aristotle had been mistaken in teaching that the velocity of falling objects was proportionate to their weight. Simon Stevin, a Dutch-man, had done this fifty years before him. But Galileo was the first to derive a mathematical proof of the true velocity of falling objects and then to devise a repeatable experiment that permitted its confirmation. If any single act made mod-ern science possible, it was this. More: it made modern sci-ence inevitable.

The three essentials of Galileo's method were abstraction, measurement, and repetition. We are so much his children that we take these for granted and fail to see their wonder. Lacking anything even remotely like a stopwatch, Galileo relied at first on counting his pulse beats in order to measure the time it took for a brass ball to roll down a groove in an inclined plane. Later he devised a sort of water clock that allowed him to measure, "with such exactness," as he said, "that the trials being many and many times repeated, they never differed any considerable matter."

The precision he obtained would have been impossible without abstraction. His "brazen ball, very hard, round, and smooth" was a physical object stripped to its essentials. It did not matter, as he wrote in *Il Saggiatore*, whether it was "white or red, bitter or sweet, sounding or mute, of a pleasant or unpleasant odor." Thus it was possible to abstract from—disregard—the sense qualities of objects and concentrate on distance and clock time, both of which are measurable, and both of which are factors in the velocity of any moving object whatever.

It also became possible to disregard the occult (that is to say, hidden) qualities of things that medieval philosophers claimed were responsible for physical changes. As Newton wrote, "To tell us that every species of thing is endowed with an occult specific quality, by which it acts and produces manifest effects, is to tell us nothing." The Newtonian laws of motion were neither special nor occult. They applied to everything, from an apple to the moon, even to the Earth itself. They were abstract, concerning distance, which was not a thing but a measure. They were, moreover, timeless. "It seems probable to me," he wrote, "that God in the beginning formed matter in solid, massy, hard, impenetrable, moveable particles . . . as most conduced to the end for which he formed them." Though Newton himself did not take the next step, it was only a short one from his belief to the Deist view of the world as a sort of giant clock that God had invented and built and wound up and left to run of its own accord in obedience to the principles He built into it.

Newton's *Mathematical Principles of Natural Philosophy* was published in 1687, and for the next two hundred-odd

years physicists and astronomers were enthusiastically occupied in tracing the works of that giant clock. Copernicus
and Galileo had deprived God of an actual place for His
Heaven; Galileo and Newton deprived Him of anything to
do. At the same time, they deprived priests of much of their
revealed authority. If an eclipse of the sun was a natural oc-
currence, it could not be cited as an expression of God's
wrath at the sinfulness of mankind. If an eclipse of the sun
was not an expression of God's wrath, it became difficult to
argue that a plague was, either, and so the way was open to
discover the roles of the rat and the flea.

iii

Medieval ethical doctrine, which included medieval economics, concerned a static society in which the proper relations of individual to individual and of individuals to God
were immutable. It was a world of six foreordained periods,
from Creation to Second Coming, to which St. Augustine
had added a seventh, the Eternal Sabbath. Though these
periods followed one after the other, they described a se-
quence, not a history. The various periods had been and
would be reached and passed regardless of what anyone did
or did not do; and what was virtuous or sinful had no relation
to any period but was from everlasting to everlasting.

During the Renaissance, the medieval ban on usury
spurred the first tentative steps in the direction of fractional-
reserve banking, which, coupled with double-entry book-
keeping, introduced a dynamism into business that was as
fateful for the static medieval world view as was the cosmology of Copernicus. After Adam Smith, economic theory,
following economic practice, became dynamic. It did so, not
by reforming its ethical base, but ultimately by denying it.

In the second chapter of *The Wealth of Nations*, Smith
announces that the "division of labor, from which so many
advantages are derived, is not originally the effect of any human wisdom. It is the necessary, though very slow and grad-

ual, consequence of a certain propensity in human nature which has in view no such extensive utility; the propensity to truck, barter, and exchange one thing for another." This is clearly the theme of impersonality, but the definitive metaphor does not yet appear.

We hear of the invisible hand in a surprising context: "By preferring the support of domestic products to that of foreign industry, [every individual] intends only his own security; and by directing that industry in such a manner as its produce may be of the greatest value, he intends only his own gain, and he is in this, as in many other cases, led by an invisible hand to promote an end which was no part of his intention. Nor is it always the worse for society that it was no part of it. By pursuing his own interest he frequently promotes that of society more effectually than he really intends to promote it. I have never known much good done by those who affected to trade for the public good. It is an affectation, indeed, not very common among merchants," Smith adds drily, "and very few words need be employed in dissuading them from it."

There are several aspects of this passage that may be astonishing. First, it comes not at the beginning of the book (where Smith put his famous analysis of the division of labor) but halfway through it, as an incidental point in an argument against import restrictions. Second, it is not stated as an immutable rule (*"Nor is it always* the worse," *"frequently,"* "I have never known *much* good"). Third, it is based on merchants' preferences (which no longer exist, if they ever did) for domestic over foreign products. Fourth, it is connected with the rest of economics only as an afterthought ("as in many other cases"). Yet the invisible hand shook the world.

Smith's less metaphorical, but perhaps as frequently cited, statement of the idea comes even further on, more than two-thirds through the book: ". . . the obvious and simple system of natural liberty establishes itself of its own accord. Every man, as long as he does not violate the laws of justice, is left perfectly free to pursue his own interest in his own way, and to bring both his industry and capital into competition with those of any other men or order of men." This comes at the end of an attack on the physiocrats. But now Smith goes on to state explicitly the factor of the idea that gave it its historical power: "The sovereign is completely discharged from a duty . . . for the proper performance of which no human wisdom or knowledge could ever be sufficient; the duty of superintending the industry of private people, and of directing it towards the employments most suitable to the interests of society."

Here Adam Smith had made the wealth of nations seem an impersonal science on the model of Newtonian physics. Thus he changed irrevocably the conditions of our thoughts and lives. His words were so simple, so elegant, so appropriate to the spirit of the times that they carried instant conviction to all who heard them. Where only a few years earlier Rousseau had declared that "Man is born free, and everywhere he is in chains," the striking off of those chains now seemed an imminent possibility. And it would be done automatically, effortlessly, by the invisible hand, now that the heavy hand of sovereign lords was seen to be unnecessary. No one any longer needed to feel guilty in challenging the inherited authority of kings or the revealed morality of priests as obligatory guides. The pursuit of self-interest would work, regardless of intention, for the benefit of all; and self-serving labor, freed of its taint of miserliness and greed, could achieve miracles of production, making use of the technical miracles of the natural sciences. The wealth of nations, which had previously been determined by military or dynastic maneuvering, could become the daily concern of commoners.

iv

By Darwin's time the scientific method developed by Galileo was carrying all before it. If every event has a cause, and if the universe is uniform, miracles are no longer sought or feared. Scientific inquiry, once fairly begun, is interminable.

If human illnesses are natural, the human body becomes a part of nature. And if the human body is natural, it would seem that the human mind, if it is human, must be natural, too.

At this point, a curious reversal occurred. It appeared early in Karl Marx, in works written fifteen years before *The Origin of Species*, though published posthumously. Like Rousseau, Marx saw mankind in chains and searched for the means of liberation. He found it in history, which to him was comprehensible only as it was lawful, and lawful only as it was impersonal and inexorable. He considered himself a materialist, and understood history to be materialist in the same way that classical physics was materialist.

Developing his ideas, he wrote: "It is not a matter of what this or that proletarian or even the proletariat as a whole *pictures* at present as its goal. It is a matter of *what the proletariat is in actuality* and what, in accordance with this *being*, it will historically be compelled to do." What was launched in search of freedom has paradoxically come aground on socio-historical compulsion. Marx was not the last to sail these waters.

We find mankind liberated from spooks and spirits, from lords and priests, by becoming mechanized. Once the universe was running like a clock, there was nothing for it but to fit us to a wheel in the works—perhaps a greater thing than a cog, but mechanical nevertheless. For us to be fit for this function, psychology had to subject us to mechanical controls. Or, as has been said, we had first to lose our souls, then our minds, and finally, with the behaviorists, consciousness.

The great economists have added their details to the description of this remarkable servomechanism. In spite of years of devoted study and ever more powerful generations of computers, model after model has had to be abandoned. The servomechanism somehow seems not to work very well. It is a puzzle.

Before directing our attention to the puzzle, we may pause a moment to note that economics is not the only field of bewilderment. Three great revolutions in physics destabilized the Newtonian world: Maxwell's dynamical theory of the electromagnetic field (1864), Einstein's special theory of relativity (1905), and Heisenberg's uncertainty principle (1926). The questions these men raised, and the solutions they put forward, are so profoundly unsettling as to suggest that what we still call the modern world may be coming to a turning point, if not to its end.

To see whether and to what extent economics is in a comparable position, we must look more closely at its presuppositions, beginning with its understanding of psychology.

2

PSYCHOLOGY

Why the Profit Motive Isn't in the Psychology Textbooks

i

In turning to psychology, we do what all the great economists have done. Adam Smith opened his first book, *The
Theory of Moral Sentiments*, with this sentence: "How self-
ish soever man may be supposed, there are evidently some
principles in his nature, which interest him in the fortunes of
others, and render their happiness necessary to him, though
he derives nothing from it except the pleasure of seeing it."
Though he used the word "evidently," he produced no evidence; yet he went on to base the theory of his book on the
"principles in his nature" that he no doubt sincerely believed
he had discovered.

The greatest economist of this century, John Maynard
Keynes, followed in his train. At a crucial point in *The General Theory of Employment, Interest and Money*, he wrote:
"The fundamental psychological law, upon which we are entitled to depend with great confidence both *a priori* from our
knowledge of human nature and from the detailed facts of
experience, is that men are disposed, as a rule and on the
average, to increase their consumption as their income increases, but not by as much as the increase in their income."
Of a lesser man than Keynes one might be tempted to say
that he wrote so emphatically because his evidence was so
slight. In any case, whatever evidence he might have had,

he adduced none; and one may scour all the psychology textbooks in the land without coming across the faintest adumbration of this allegedly dependable psychological law.

The psychology invoked by economists has, it must be acknowledged, borne little relation to that studied by psychologists. This anomaly was noted as long ago as 1925 by Wesley Clair Mitchell, a founder of the National Bureau of Economic Research, who made what must be judged a preliminary and superficial attempt to tie his economics to the then-fashionable behaviorist psychology of John B. Watson.

Economics had to come to ground somewhere. Almost universally, the ground chosen or assumed has been self-interest, an apparently simple, straightforward, and obvious concept. It is, nevertheless, easier to understand what is meant by the idea of self-interest or the pleasure-pain principle than to use the idea in furthering understanding. Galileo's brass ball rolled in the same way, accelerating in the same way, every time he released it at the top of his inclined plane. But regardless of Adam Smith's notion of a propensity to barter, sometimes a deal goes through, and sometimes it doesn't. One person will see self-interest in a swap, and the next won't. This seems, so to say, perfectly natural. They're different people. Everyone is different. People are differently endowed and come from different backgrounds and have different needs, wants, hopes, expectations, fears, understandings, interests. Everyone is strange but me and thee.

In all honesty, human beings behave very strangely indeed. With the reports of thousands of cultural anthropologists before us, we know that there is scarcely a practice commonly seen in one part of the world that is not shunned in another. Even in Smith's day enough was known of the customs of the Chinese and the American Indians and, nearer at hand, some sadly disreputable Frenchmen, to understand that their behavior differed from that of a Scottish scholar who lived much of his life with his mother.

What, then, becomes of human nature? If people act differently because they *are* different, what is gained by claiming they are of the same nature because they act out of self-interest? Self-interest would appear to be as various as humanity. There's no disputing over tastes. One man's meat is another man's poison. There's no pleasing some people. Is there such a thing as self-interest, after all?

The usual answer to this question says that it's *enlightened* self-interest that is really uniform. The form of the answer appears again and again in the history of Western thought and again and again as a proposed solution to economic problems.

The distinction between self-interest and enlightened self-interest seems the same as the familiar distinction between appearance and reality. We are used to mistrusting the appearance of things; it is prudent to look for the underlying or hidden reality. "Things are seldom what they seem," sings Little Buttercup in *Pinafore*, "Skim milk masquerades as cream." Nor is this search merely a question of prudence; it is also a mark of wisdom. It is a major theme of most, if not all, religions, which celebrate the superior reality of some world other than this, or the superior force of some supernatural power. It is a recurring concern of poets, who probe with Wordsworth "something far more deeply interfused," with Eliot "the world of perpetual solitude."

The notion of the underlying reality of enlightened self-interest is the very model of an *a priori* judgment. It assumes what it pretends to prove. It claims that we would behave in a certain way if we knew what's good for us. If we don't behave in the prescribed way, it's because we don't know what's good for us. There is no way of attacking or even defending this form of argument.

Enlightened self-interest is a dogma no more successful in subduing the riot of human behavior than is self-interest without the enlightenment. Neither can make anything of a man like St. Francis. Was he bartering for his soul when he shed his raiment and renounced his inheritance? What were his worldly contemporaries doing when they bought and sold indulgences? Which of these were enlightened and which misguided cannot be determined by examining their success in reaching their objectives or by assaying the pleasure they enjoyed. It would be preposterous to claim that Gandhi led the Satyagraha in order to enjoy mundane comfort; it would also be preposterous to claim that, had he been enlightened, he would not have led it.

Self-interest as the profit motive is frankly a form of self-ishness or greed. Samuel Johnson was willing to say that "There are few ways in which a man can be more innocently employed than in getting money," but sharp practice is not so innocent. While no one praises greed as such, many somehow think that economics can bend it to its purposes.

This is an uncommon state of affairs in the history of civilization and its discontents. In most other cases where a motive is identified, the motive or drive or instinct is judged vicious in its natural state and only becomes beneficent under restraint, if then. Thus unbridled lust would destroy society; so society seeks to control it, not to encourage it. "It is better to marry than to burn," said St. Paul. By its recognition of marriage, society transforms lust into caring and responsibility, if not into love. Even a frequently useful drive, like aggressiveness, is not encouraged to advance to assault, battery, and murder. Many are tempted by the rewards of thievery; some find difficulty in telling the truth, even under oath. These are recognized disorders, and we restrain them with legal sanctions. But the profit motive is assiduously encouraged.

The formlessness of the profit motive is underlined by its inability to say what cannot be allowed in its pursuit. The rule of *caveat emptor* is favored because it eases the way of the maker of profits. Some say slavery is inefficient but are still content to recommend the indirect coercion of starvation. Dangerous working conditions that amount to mayhem and manslaughter seem to be not unacceptable if safety measures threaten to interfere with profit making.

ii

The most thoroughgoing statement of the notion of self-interest was made by the British utilitarians under the leadership of Jeremy Bentham. "By the principle of utility," he wrote in 1789, "is meant that principle which approves or disapproves of every action whatsoever, according to the tendency which it appears to have to augment or diminish the happiness of the party whose interest is in question." In furtherance of this principle, Bentham devoted much thought to the elaboration of a "felicific calculus," whereby pleasures and pains could be judged and appropriate choices made. This, surely one of the most curious by-ways in the history of thought, was intended to do for morals what Newton had done for motion.

We need notice only how quickly Bentham's calculations were forced to abandon their intended objectivity. The evaluation of pains and pleasures inevitably depended upon the person doing the valuing, and that person had to be the one experiencing the pleasures and pains. This Bentham himself insisted in his aphorism "Quantity of pleasure being equal, [the game of] pushpin is as good as poetry." Pierre Dumont, a Swiss friend and disciple, put it more prosaically: "Everyone will constitute himself judge of his own utility; this is and ought to be, otherwise man would not be a reasonable being." In an introduction to Bentham's work, J. H. Burton concluded that Bentham defined pleasure so that "what it pleases a man to do is simply what he wills to do." Thus self-interest becomes self-assertion.

iii

It is commonly said that the test of self-interest is the maximization of material gains. It is no trick at all to show the hopelessness of trying to apply the test. In what period of time are the gains to be maximized? Surely immediate maximization is not meant, nor would it be useful to say, as Herodotus quotes Solon as saying, that no one can be happy except looking back over his entire life in the hour of his death. So an intermediate-term gain must be the objective. But how long would an intermediate term be? And what is a material gain? Does only the amassing of money count? (As we shall see, money isn't material, anyhow.) Again, is it in your interest to put money in your purse at the cost of the friendship or the well-being of others? If not, why not? On the premises of the test, there is no way of saying why not. Or is it in your interest to spend all your energy in amassing wealth and none in spending it? Of course, it would be absurd to be so miserly, but there's nothing in the test that says it's absurd; that judgment, too, comes from elsewhere.

And of course one must be reasonable in applying any test. The essence of reasonableness is giving reasons. What reasons are to be given, and what is their authority? By being reasonable does one merely intend something like the golden mean: nothing to excess, as the inscription on the Delphinian Temple of Apollo had it? Then what is excessive? If you make a million, why not strive for two? Or *must* you? Two million might not be an all-absorbing task for you, and two billion might be child's play for an oil baron, but two thousand or even two hundred might be an impossible limit for someone less fortunately positioned. Is excess then to be judged on an individual basis? If so, are we not back to the realization that every individual is different? Yet this was the conclusion we tried to escape by introducing the notion of enlightened self-interest.

Some have proposed that self-interest be linked to need, and it used to be said that the economic needs are food, clothing, and shelter. But it is well known to nutritionists that Americans, at any rate, eat too much. A need may be established for one suit of clothes, but whence comes the need for a second? And who really needs as large a dwelling as he or she now occupies—or a "vacation home" at all? Lear understood the question: "O, reason not the need! . . . Allow not nature more than nature needs, Man's life is cheap as beast's." Or as Hamlet had it: "What is a man, if his chief use and market of his time be but to sleep and feed? A beast: no more." If only physiological needs are allowed, the birds of the air are economists. If psychological needs are admitted, we are again back either to the riot of individuality or to the imposition of some arbitrary standard.

Similar difficulties will attend any other empirical test of self-interest. Every attempt to establish such a definition ends either in confusion or in dogma. Either we must confess we can't tell what self-interest is or we must settle on some nonempirical definition.

Downright commonsensical people—today's Samuel Johnsons—may well be irritated by all this logic-chopping. They have little or no doubt as to where their interests lie. They have no time for anguished hand-wringing. Winning is the only thing, and they get on with it. They think we'd be well advised to get on with it, too. In real life, which is not a game, they quickly become tongue-tied if we ask them what they mean by winning; nevertheless, they may have something to teach us. For if they are sure where their interests lie, it is because they define them. They are their interests, and no one else's, because they say what they are.

And this is, in the end, true of all of us. Our interests are what we say they are; our motives are what we say they are. We are what we say our interests are. To be sure, there are hypocrites and deceivers among us; that is not the problem, for they have their own standards even though they keep them hidden from the rest of us or even from themselves. It is also true that we are all more or less clumsy, blind, counterproductive in furthering the interests we acknowledge, that we are all our own worst enemies, that we are all more or less surprised and dissatisfied with the outcomes. The surprise is not part of the problem but part of the solution. All action is more or less blind. What's to come is still unsure.

The stumbling block to an empirical definition of self-interest is not the idea of interest but the idea of self. Self is autonomous or it is nothing. No respect in which we are identical with one another makes us autonomous. Montague is nor hand, nor foot, nor arm, nor face, nor any other part belonging to a man. What identifies Romeo is what he says and does: "Call me but love, and I'll be new baptized." He asserts himself.

Empiricism discovers what things have in common. Whatever is green is to that extent like other green things; whatever is heavy is like other heavy things; whatever is cold is like other cold things. Whatever is green, heavy, and cold is like other green, heavy, and cold things. Add whatever predicates strike your fancy and however many you can list, and you will still describe how a thing is like something else. That is what predicates do.

Yet we are alike in our selfhood. Diogenes Laërtius tells a story, undoubtedly apocryphal, to the effect that Plato defined man as a featherless biped, whereupon Diogenes the Cynic plucked a chicken and tossed it before the Academy, prompting the modification "with broad flat nails." Since one-legged people are not uncommon, and no-legged and no-fingered people not unknown, some of them even having been born that way, the definition fails to define. One can do better with Aristotle's observation that man is a rational animal.

Rationality is a curious concept, nearer than hands and feet. It implies responsibility, an acceptance of the consequences of thought, a willingness to give reasons and to act on them. No one is responsible for anything he is forced to do or over which he has no control. Responsibility implies autonomy, and we are again back to the failure of an empirical approach to self, and consequently to the failure of an empirical approach to self-interest.

The search for human nature masks another problem. If there were such a nature, the possibility of changing it would be foreclosed. Conservatives pretend to shudder at Marx's dictum "The philosophers have only *interpreted* the world, in various ways; the point, however, is to *change* it." But most social scientists, reactionary as well as radical, carry a blueprint for a braver world in their knapsacks. The blueprints, whether explicitly or implicitly, assume a change in human nature, which is expected to become more altruistic or egotistic or socially conscious or whatever may be required.

It is nevertheless claimed that economics is based on a constancy, if not on a constant. The constancy is the theory that human beings always want more—more of the same thing or

more of other things. Since money can buy other things, it is
argued that human beings always want more money.

On the physiological level, there is no doubt that the food
I consume today won't sustain me long after tomorrow; I'll
need more. On neither day, however, will I eat everything I
can lay my hands on. After a day at an amusement park, I
may never want to see cotton candy again. There are limits
to my appetite for any particular food and for food in general, and there are limits to all my appetites, severally and
collectively. The limits may be very broad, and they may
very well be subject to fantastic stretching by my passion to
keep up with my neighbors, but there are actual limits, and
I am the one who sets the limits. Buffeted by peer pressure
though I am, seduced by advertising, overwhelmed by child-
hood memories, in spite of all I reach actual limits, and they
are where I say they are. The saying may be desperate or
joyful; it may be unplanned and even unconscious; but it is
mine, not yours. We are back to self-assertion.

iv

It should be added that the psychological approach to economics has not succeeded even on its own premises. Though
self-interest must seem protean in any attempt at empirical
definition, it is always arbitrarily and narrowly construed
when applied to the affairs of the world. The argument says
that people do economic things only for profit, and that
therefore the way to get them to do things is to make the
doing profitable, that is, immediately and lavishly rewarded
with money. This has always been the rationale of conservative economics and is by no means the invention of our
contemporary conservatives. What follows, of course, is that
greed becomes a virtue, albeit not openly acknowledged as
such. And that is a terrible thing to say.

It is also a terrible thing to select as the ground of public
policy. If you encourage greed, you will surely discover a
great deal of it hitherto hidden under stones. Greed is,

moreover, in the end an ineffectual basis for public policy. That is to say, it is ineffectual if your ultimate aim is something other than more greed. It may even be true that most men and women are mostly motivated by greed. But many, in a long line from Socrates to Mother Teresa, are not. So when you attempt to run your economy on greed, you're running on comparatively few cylinders, and not necessarily the best ones.

Similar failure will plague you no matter what psychological motive you select to base your economics on. Karl Marx hoped to release the creative and productive instincts of mankind by devising an economy in which it would be "possible for me to do one thing today and another tomorrow, to hunt in the morning, fish in the afternoon, rear cattle in the evening, criticize after dinner, just as I have a mind, without ever becoming hunter, fisherman, cowboy, or critic." Herbert Marcuse thought that this notorious passage from *The German Ideology*, written in 1846, was a joke, and others have thought it a young man's aberration. But the same notion appears thirty years later in *Critique of the Gotha Program*, where Marx announces that in the communist future, production will not be a problem, because it will have "increased with the all-around development of the individual." Mao's China, during the Great Proletarian Cultural Revolution, made an attempt to reduce Marx's vision to practice. The results were not remarkably satisfactory, from any point of view.

While it might consequently occur to a commonsensical person to question the premises of greed or creativity on which these various programs were based, the point here is that motivation is the wrong idea, anyhow. It suggests what people do automatically, what they are programmed to do. In so far as psychology inquires into such doings, it is no longer a suitable foundation for political economy. It played a historical role in helping to free us from absolute kings. But the issue now is not freedom from, but freedom, that is, autonomy.

*

v

Nothing in the foregoing denies (or affirms) the validity of any proposition in psychology or the virtue of the study of psychology. Every human action can be studied from the points of view of all the arts and sciences. Nothing I do is without physical aspect; there is never a time when I do not obey the laws of motion, when I can step off a moving train without experiencing a rude, but equal and opposite, reaction. Nothing I do is ever without physiological aspect. If you prick me, I will bleed, and the blood will fall to the ground at the rate of $S = \frac{1}{2}gt^2$. Nothing I do is without emotional content, and your assault will make me angry or sad. Nor is there anything I do that is in principle non-economic: if I stay home to nurse my wound, I'll also suffer a loss of income. But the velocity of the fall of my blood is irrelevant to my loss of income.

Just as it would be a confusion of terms to say that the attraction of positive and negative charges for each other is an expression of love, or that the stars in their courses reveal the greatness of Beethoven, so it is a confusion of terms to search for psychological explanations of economic events. There is, however, one discipline that seems a special case: mathematics, if only because economics seems always to involve numbers. In the modern world, the authority of mathematics has rivaled the authority of psychology. That authority must now be examined.

3

MATHEMATICS

Why Physics Is Value Free and Economics Isn't

i

Galileo, on the basis of a few almost casual observations, proposed a mathematical formula for the velocity of any falling body, excluding all sorts of irrelevant data, and then devised measurable experiments that confirmed the formula. In the same way, Newton combined the astronomical findings and theories of Copernicus and Kepler with Galileo's formula to produce universal laws of motion. He then sought observations that would confirm these laws. At first he failed, and put his study aside. The story goes that fifteen years later, working with new figures, he became so excited as he saw confirmation looming that he had to call in a friend to finish the calculations. This is the model: observation, abstraction, deduction, measurement, confirmation.

In the social sciences an early, if not the first, work along these lines was done by John Graunt, a haberdasher and captain of militia, who studied the mortality records of the City of London and prepared what he called a "Table showing one hundred quick conceptions, how many die within six years, how many the next decade, and so for every decade till 76." His work appeared in 1661, twenty-six years before Newton's *Principia*. Graunt evidently prepared his table for fun, but it was quickly taken up by the nascent insurance business, and a general statement of the principles behind such work was made by Sir William Petty, a friend of Graunt's.

Because of this statement, Petty is credited as one of the founders of modern statistics, which he called political arithmetic, and which he defined as "the art of reasoning by figures upon things relating to the government." Petty was a minor sort of Renaissance man, a professor of anatomy at Oxford, the organizer of the survey of Cromwell's grants of land in Ireland, a landlord himself of some fifty thousand acres in County Kerry, and an occasional essayist on economic subjects. A longish essay or short book, published posthumously because it contained references to France offensive to Petty's patron Charles II, was *Five Discourses on Political Arithmetic*. "The method I use," Petty wrote, "is not yet very usual; for, instead of using only comparative and superlative words, and intellectual arguments, I have taken the course . . . to express myself in terms of number, weight, and measure; to use only arguments of sense, and to consider only such causes as have visible foundations in nature."

One would think that, with Graunt and Petty and, in addition, several others on the Continent, economics was well under way on a course parallel to that of astronomy and physics. It is therefore with something of a shock that we listen to Adam Smith pronouncing a full hundred years later, "I have no great faith in political arithmetic."

What had gone wrong?

The biographical reason for Smith's rejection of political arithmetic no doubt turned on his vehement rejection of mercantilism, one of the principal themes of his book. Petty, like others of his time, was a mercantilist. Though it is most unlikely that Smith had not read Petty's work, and it is certain that he was aware of the discipline Petty had named, yet Petty himself is not named in *The Wealth of Nations*. This is surprising because, as Robert Heilbroner notes, over a hundred authors are referred to by name in Smith's treatise.

Personality aside, the episode would seem to suggest some reason to be wary of statistics in economics. Smith had what seemed to him, and still seem to us two centuries later, sound reasons for opposing the Corn Laws. These reasons owed nothing to the figures that had been collected, even though they were in Smith's favor. "I mention them," he said, "only to show of how much less consequence in the opinion of most judicious and experienced persons, the foreign trade of corn is than the home trade." He refused to bother himself about the accuracy of the figures, and thought they proved nothing except the size of the problem. By the same token, the figures that evidently persuaded others, including Petty, of the merits of mercantilism, carried no conviction to Smith.

This sort of thing still goes on. In the past hundred years we have collected unbelievable quantities of statistics on everything one can imagine, especially on all aspects of economic life. The annual "Economic Report of the President" is thought to need 125 pages of statistics to support about the same amount of text. Yet that report is subject to vituperative debate within the establishment and to withering scorn from outside. It is commonplace—even expected— that economists will agree on figures and will debate irreconcilably about their meaning.

A situation like this does not occur in the natural sciences. Once Simon Stevin showed that the velocities of falling bodies are not proportionate to their weight, no student continued to hold Aristotle's side of the question. Newton was no doubt dismayed when his first calculations failed to demonstrate the inverse-square law. He may even have suspected that the figure he had been given for the radius of the earth was wrong. But he did not pretend that the figure didn't matter, that the law held regardless of the figure.

Why should economists behave differently? Surely it cannot be that only irresponsible and cantankerous fools take up economics, while selfless, reasonable, and truth-seeking men and women go into the natural sciences. There are too many on both sides who find no role in such a scenario. While Darwin was a mild man, Huxley certainly was not. While Marx was disputatious, Cantillon was retiring. Nor can the

difference between the disciplines be merely passing functions of the intellectual climate, for the differences existed in
Smith's day and they continue in ours. The record strongly
suggests a fundamental difference between natural and social
science. General acceptance of some difference is of course
indicated by the usual division of the sciences into the two
broad classifications, with physics always in one group, and
economics always in the other.

"Number, weight, and measure" will not actually take one
very far in economics. One may no doubt count the bushels
of wheat each farmer grows and then add the output of all
the wheat farmers in the land to get the national output. And
one can do the same for tons of coal and for almost anything
produced by farming or mining. One can even classify and
total the types and grades of steel produced by steel mills.
Thereafter things get much more complicated. Some steel
goes into stovepipes and some into cannons, some into
bridge girders and some into snuff boxes. A pine forest may
yield ships' spars, residential clapboarding, and paper products. Tables of the numbers, weights, and measures of these
products may be of interest to individual producers, but they
are too diverse for inferences of any generality. You cannot,
as the saying goes, add apples and pears.

It should, moreover, be noted that to divide fruit into apples and pears, even to separate fruit from steel girders, is
illicit on the premises of political arithmetic. An apple and a
needle both have number, weight, and measure and therefore, on the premises, should be added together. Carry it a
step further: it is illicit on the premises to distinguish a good
apple from a rotten one or a potato from the dirt that is
turned up when it is harvested. Newtonian mechanics works
as well with a rotten apple as with a good one, but it would
appear that economics may be somehow different.

ii

A strong statement in favor of mathematical thinking was
made by William Stanley Jevons, a logician and economist,
who argued in 1871 that *our science must be mathematical,*

simply because it deals with quantities. Wherever the things treated are capable of being *greater or less,* there the laws and relations must be mathematical in nature." [Jevons's emphases.] His point, Jevons insists, is not merely that mathematical notation is used, because "If we had no regard to trouble and prolixity, the most complicated mathematical problems might be stated in ordinary language." Rather, he holds that "There can be but two classes of sciences—those which are *simply logical,* and *those which, besides being logical, are also mathematical.*" A logical science "determines whether a thing be or not be . . . but if the thing may be greater or less, or the event may happen sooner or later, nearer or farther, then quantitative notions enter."

As so often happens in the history of thought, Jevons claims both too little and too much. The sort of question he assigns exclusively to logic—to be or not to be—is not merely characteristic of Hamlet but is also the basis of computer circuitry and so is the mathematics *par excellence* of our day. On the other hand, very little of logic is as restricted as Jevons suggests. The universal affirmative proposition of the form "All apples are fruits" certainly seems to meet his standard. But this proposition may be converted by immediate inference to the particular affirmative "Some fruits are apples," which is something else. Whatever is particular—"some"—may be counted.

In any case, it by no means follows that all "sciences" that deal in quantities are merely mathematical. As a matter of fact, the obvious exceptions to Jevons's rule are legion, from penology to pharmacology. Criminals are sentenced to prison for a number of days or years, or are required to pay a fine of a number of dollars; but no one supposes that judges do or should turn to mathematicians for advice in imposing sentence. Likewise, it is usual to prescribe ten grains of aspirin for a headache, but the prescription does not appear in any mathematics text.

Coming at the question from another direction, we find that Jevons's claim is much less comprehensive than it may seem. Trigonometry is a part of mathematics, and the law of sines is a part of trigonometry, but the application of the law of sines to economics does not appear. Not all of mathematics is relevant to economics; yet if any branch is irrelevant, the relevance of every branch must be shown. It cannot be assumed. And the showing must—unless it begs the question—be based on meta-mathematical standards, that is, on standards that include both mathematics and economics.

Nor are only relatively specialized branches of mathematics in question. The task of algebra is to explore the relationship between dependent and independent variables. A decision as to which are dependent and which independent must be made to get the equation into usable form. One may debate whether the interest rate depends on the rate of inflation, or vice versa; and not only the shape of the equation but the deduced policy recommendations will be at stake. And there is a still prior question: Do the given variables have a dependent/independent relationship at all? Or, if they sometimes have such a relationship, is it regular?

The answer to this question is by no means obvious or automatic. We may, for example, brush aside as frivolous Jevons's proposed connections between sunspots and the stock market, but an astronomer as distinguished as Harlan Stetson took the matter seriously enough to write a book about it. The illustration is more sharply focused by the fact that shortly after he wrote his book Stetson joined in the furious attack on Immanuel Velikovsky's best-selling quasi-literal interpretation of Biblical cosmology.

The point is that neither the sunspot question nor the Biblical question is definitively answered by mathematics. One can of course make errors in any mathematical calculation, and such errors certainly vitiate the conclusion; but mathematical correctness is no guarantee of a meaningful answer. Stetson rejected Velikovsky, not because of faulty mathematics, but because if Velikovsky were right the entire structure of modern science would crumble. More than astronomy was at risk, because astronomy is consistent with physics, and physics with chemistry, and chemistry with biology. In the same way, economics must be consistent with ethics in the broad sense and with all humanistic concerns, nor may humanism be inconsistent with natural science if our life is to be intelligible.

Although the law of sines has not been thought to have an economics application, a great deal of contemporary economics leans heavily on trigonometry and analytic geometry. A curious fact about the rank jungle of multicolored curves choking the pages of the textbooks is that numbers rarely attach to them; and when numerical values are represented, they often turn out to be estimated or wholly imaginary—a schedule showing the supposed (or denied) price elasticity of wheat, the kinked oligopoly demand curve, and so on. In almost all cases no one knows what the actual figures may be; the given figures are assumed in order to illustrate a theory.

This is a matter of some practical importance. The problem lies not in the fact that the actual numbers are truly difficult to come by or even, in some instances, impossible to come by. No one has been to the interior of the sun; yet astrophysicists talk confidently of what goes on there. This is possible because natural science is a unified structure. What the astrophysicist can observe about the sun can occur only if what he theorizes about the interior is true. Hence it *is* true. Revisions of course occur every day, but the system stands. The textbooks talk as though a similar system works in economics, but actually it does not. Every business—especially every one selling by mail—has experimented with price changes and found instances where a price increase has increased sales. Nothing like this happens in natural science, where there never are exceptions supposed to prove the rule.

iii

In the same article in which Wesley Clair Mitchell called for an alliance between economics and behaviorist psychology, he also urged a shift from qualitative to quantitative work.

"Our qualitative theory," he wrote, "has followed the logic of Newtonian mechanics. . . . In the hedonistic calculus which Jevons followed, man is placed under the governance of two sovereign masters, pain and pleasure, which play the same role in controlling human behavior that Newton's laws of motion play in controlling the behavior of the heavenly bodies. . . . The mechanical view involves the notions of sameness, of certainty, of invariant laws; the statistical view [introduced by Clerk-Maxwell] involves the notions of variety, of probability, of approximations."

This odd analogy invites a couple of comments. First, there is no qualitative/quantitative split between Newton and Maxwell: they are both quantitative through and through. And, as we have seen, Jevons was as enthusiastic a supporter of quantitative methods in economics as anyone since. Nor was he unaware of the fact that the numbers he worked with were imprecise. "Many persons," he observed, "entertain a prejudice against mathematical language, arising out of a confusion between the ideas of a mathematical science and an exact science . . . but in reality, there is no such thing as an exact science, except in a comparative sense. Astronomy is more exact than other sciences, because the position of a planet or star admits of close measurement; but, if we examine the methods of physical astronomy, we find that they are all approximate. . . . Had physicists waited until their data were perfectly precise before they brought in the aid of mathematics, we should have still been in the age of science which terminated in the time of Galileo." This debater's point could serve Mitchell as well.

A second and more important comment on Mitchell is that the world of Maxwell, Einstein, and Heisenberg is no less subject to invariant laws than is the world of Newton. In physics, to be sure, the detailed precision of optics is confined to relatively gross phenomena, such as the refraction of a beam of light upon hitting a body of water. In a given experiment, the intensity of the beam and the angle of refraction never vary regardless of the date of the experiment or the name of the experimenter. But whether a particular photon will be refracted or reflected cannot be said: the beam is the statistical result of a lot of photons. So far, so good. But nothing that can be said about a particular photon is in conflict with what can be said about gross phenomena. On the contrary, explanation of gross phenomena allows for, and must allow for, the diverse behavior of determinate and regular proportions of photons. It does not happen that today 10 percent of the photons are reflected, though yesterday, under identical conditions, 20 percent were reflected, while the day before the figure was 12. One would scarcely know how to grind and coat lenses in such an unreliable world, which would always be more or less out of focus.

A key phrase, of course, is "under identical conditions." We have, however, already seen that conditions for self-interested economic agents are *never* identical. The behavior that economists try to describe statistically is in fact in constant flux. Indeed, it is exactly this shifting of demand and supply from here to there, from high to low, from this to that, that is supposed to be measured by the market. The "market" of a beam of light is constant; the economic market is forever unstable. As Sir Thomas Browne said of the song the Sirens sang, the explanation of the market's rise and fall is not beyond all conjecture. But such explanation will not be of the same order as the explanations of optics.

iv

Business nevertheless depends upon numbers. Not only does every firm have routine procedures for estimating costs and sales, neither of which can be precisely known in advance, but every firm must be constantly evaluating its assets, both for its internal purposes and for its relations with tax authorities and other creditors. Some firms carry good will as an asset; most do not. Inventory may be valued at historical cost (FIFO: first in, first out) or at replacement cost (LIFO: last in, first out), neither of which has any necessary relation to eventual sales price or, especially, to what the inventory might bring in a forced liquidation. Nor is it unusual for a firm to use different valuations for different purposes: in inflationary times, FIFO makes management look good, while LIFO holds down tax liability; in deflationary times, vice versa. And so on.

Since these business practices compare comparable values, they are different in an important way from the supposed operation of the felicific calculus. There is no intelligible way of comparing my pleasure in reading Keynes with Keynes's pleasure in watching the ballet. No theory can be erected on the fact or even the alleged intensity of these pleasures, and no general consequence flows from them. But given generally accepted accounting practices, as the cant phrase has it, the profitability of various firms can be compared, and so can the relative profitability, within the firm, of competing program proposals.

There is also an important difference between the method of accounting and that of the natural sciences. A business may, as Friedrich von Wieser argued, impute values to the factors of production in order to decide what to do. But physics would collapse if scientists merely imputed the number of electrons in an atom of hydrogen or the velocity of a falling object. To be sure, physics often has to hypostatize, or guess, what it is up to, but the guess is the beginning, not the end. More important, the guess will be used for all purposes, as will the refined value that ultimately replaces it. But the value assigned to a business asset is defined by the purpose of the valuation—more precisely, by the purpose of the evaluator—and is not necessarily useful for any other purpose.

v

The attraction of mathematics for economists is no doubt enhanced (as Jevons suggests) by the hope that somewhere, somehow, they will discover something similar to Newton's inverse-square law. At first glance, Newton's problem and the econometricians' problem do seem similar. Both are confronted by a world of infinite detail and variety, and both are sustained by the hope that, somewhere in that blooming, buzzing confusion, orderly and reliable laws may be discovered. In fact, Newton experienced the order and reliability every moment of his life and could not—literally—have taken a step otherwise. The notorious apple neither flew away erratically nor disintegrated in midair, but fell solidly, as anyone would expect.

The orderly reliability of nature not only is free of the invocations of priests but also is free of the hopes and fears of ordinary men, including the scientists who study it. Experiments will come out however they come out, naturally, regardless of the intentions of the experimenters. In fact, if an experimenter is discovered to have influenced the result, the experiment is discredited, and he is disgraced.

It is not, however, the impartiality of the experimenter or observer that distinguishes natural science from social science. If social scientists report what they wished they found rather than what they did find, they are as surely discredited as are natural scientists who falsify their data. It is in their different subject matters that the difference between natural science and social science lies. Physics is value free because electrons know no value. The events reported by social scientists are not value free because the human beings who act in these events have values. By acting this way rather than that, they declare that they judge this way to be better—that is, more valuable. *Both* natural scientists and social scientists may incidentally reveal their personal values in their writings, but a report of human action will *always* concern the values of the human actors.

The world of physics is a world of abstractions discovered by human beings, but it does not depend on human beings for its operation. Distance and clock time are not values; it makes no sense to approve or disapprove of them; Margaret Fuller could not refuse to accept the universe. It is a fact that the chemical bond works in the way Linus Pauling discovered, and neither Linus Pauling nor anyone else can change it.

No value appears in the physical description of an object. A physical description defines an object that obeys physical laws, not an economic object obeying economic laws, whatever they may be. A physical description of the piece of green-backed paper in my pocket does not reveal what makes it money or what money does. Any good that I buy with my money will obey physical law, but that fact is not what will make it a good. Every service that is performed must rely on physical law, but that fact does not explain what is economic about it. *Every* object is a physical object, and *any* object may come to be an economic object; but only *some* objects are actually economic objects. Whether or not a particular object becomes an economic object depends upon what human beings do with it.

Money, goods, and services are human values. Economic production and consumption are human activities. The consumption of food is essential to life, but that fact is in biology and says nothing about the price of apples. You may be convinced that apples are physiologically better for you than acorns, and your conviction may affect the price you are willing to pay; but it is only the price that is an economic concern.

As distance and clock time are fundamental physical concepts, money, goods, and services are fundamental economic concepts. Both lists can be extended, but one distinction will always separate them: the former are value free, while the latter are value bound. If it made a difference to the laws of physics what Linus Pauling (or anyone) felt about electrons, physics would collapse. If it didn't make a difference how much money Linus Pauling (or someone) would pay for an electron microscope, either the microscope would not be an economic good, or economics would collapse.

Economics is not value free, and no amount of abstraction can make it value free. The econometricians' search for equations that will explain the economy is forever doomed to frustration. It is often said that their models don't work because, on the one hand, the variables are too many and, on the other, the statistical data are too sparse. But the physical world is as various as the economic world (they are, to repeat, both infinite) and Newton had fewer data and less powerful means of calculation than are at the disposal of Jan Tinbergen and his econometrician followers. The difference is fundamental, and the failure to understand it reduces much of modern economics to a game that unfortunately has serious consequences.

vi

After a couple of pages of moderately abstruse mathematics, Keynes remarks, "I do not myself attach much value to manipulations of this kind; . . . they involve just as much tacit assumption as to what values are taken as independent . . . as ordinary discourse does, whilst I doubt if they carry us further than ordinary discourse can." Alfred Marshall, Keynes's early mentor, wrote in the introduction to his influential textbook that "it seems doubtful whether any one spends his time well in reading lengthy translations of economic doctrines into mathematics."

To these sentiments may be added the observation that mathematics derives power not only from the conciseness of its notation but also from its stability. Whatever x may be, it is the same at the end of the exercise as it was in the beginning. Such stability is essential in thinking about the natural world, where historical time is irrelevant, and whatever happens can be replicated. In the world of economics, on the other hand, historical time is of the essence, and the essence of historical time is that it is not replicated. In physics $S = \frac{1}{2}gt^2$ is precise and immutable. But Keynes's "Aggregate Demand Function" merely states that the proceeds which entrepreneurs expect to receive is a function of the number of men they employ. It does not say what that function is, nor can it do so, for sometimes entrepreneurs expect more and sometimes less. But when the function is written $D = f(N)$, it looks precise and immutable. The very virtue of mathematical thinking disqualifies it for thinking about the fundamental issues of economics.

4

AUTONOMY

Why You Can Mean What You Say

i

In the two preceding chapters we have seen how self-interest yields to self-assertion and the impersonality of numbers yields to values that are somehow rooted in persons. These are not trivial results. People take the center of the stage and they do so as autonomous persons, not as specialized organisms whose nature is to behave according to certain rules, nor yet as entities obedient in some essential way to mathematical or physical formulae.

Autonomy is not possible in a state of nature. All attempts to define mankind in jungle terms are more or less elaborate exercises in anachronism, taking more or less educated contemporary people and setting them down in a jungle to see what they will do. Such people are not naked apes but the product and beneficiary of a long history; they are not the creatures of a jungle environment. Robinson Crusoe was an Englishman far from home, not a savage with a gun and an old nanny goat. There was no way he could not be an Englishman except by laboriously becoming something else, and that something else would not be a child of nature. Not even Friday was a child of nature.

If not children of nature, what were they? Children of some sort of society, of course: a family, a band, a tribe, perhaps a nation. A society is extended in two dimensions—

34

spatially and temporally. The extent of the dimensions sets limits—or provides opportunities, which is the same thing—for the society's members. The temporal dimension is history, including its subdivision, biography.

The case for history is the same as the case against it. The case against history argues that since the past controls the present, since the antecedents of the present can be discovered, since the present is continuous with the past, the present was really complete in the womb of time. The future, too, was likewise complete. This is a theme well known to poets and philosophically inclined scientists, and readily developed. "Given the distribution of the masses and velocities of all the material particles of the universe at any one instant of time," wrote Laplace, "it is theoretically possible to foretell their precise arrangement at any future time."

This view seems at least to grant significance to the past. It would appear that the more I can learn about the past—even though my knowledge will hardly approach that required by Laplace—the better I can understand the present and foretell the future. It is, however, all a sham; for though I foretell the future, I can do nothing about it. The future was foreordained, as was my knowledge of the past and my understanding of the present. Knowledge of this sort is not power. On the one side, it is not mine at all but was in effect dictated to me by the same process that arranged the other particles, and on the other it cannot be used for good or ill, because nothing can be changed. It is hard to say what it is, but it obviously is not an aspect of autonomy.

Does autonomy then require denial of the significance of the past? Many say so. Men of action like Henry Ford call history bunk; it was fashionable in the 1960s to call it irrelevant; professional educators scorn attention to dates; and inspirational writers urge us to consider each day the first of the rest of our lives, advising us to put the past behind us, to forget it. Denial of the past reduces life to an alleged series of instants, each of which is the first in the rest of our lives. But the alleged series never appears as a series. The past is denied, and tomorrow never comes; so there is only the instantaneous and unrelated present. The situation is like that of the arrow in Zeno's paradox, which didn't move because at each instant it was where it was and not somewhere else. Nevertheless arrows do move, as St. Sebastian is our witness. If arrows move in spite of Zeno, perhaps there is an opening for us and our autonomy.

Such an opening is sometimes sought in the interstices of the warp of compulsion and the woof of chaos, where for the past half century Heisenberg's uncertainty principle has seemed to offer a space for lawlessness within the frame of order.

Lawlessness, however, is a bit of chaos, no matter how framed. Wherever a bit of chaos may be found, nothing of any effect can be found or done. The uncertainty principle in fact points in a different direction. It states that of any particular electron, you can say either where it is, or how fast it is going, but not both, because the act of measurement will have large and unpredictable effects. "If the position of the electron is known exactly," as Max Planck says, "its velocity is not known at all, and vice versa." Science has nothing to say about particular electrons or, consequently, about particular or unique objects or events. This is no new discovery. The glory of science has been its success in discovering natural laws, and a law describes what an event has in common with other events. But whatever an event has in common with others is precisely what is not unique about it.

ii

The way I define myself will dictate the outcome of my search for autonomy. If I start searching in a state of nature, whether nasty or benign, I will, at every crucial point, find my norm to be an irresponsible existence. If I start in the Garden of Eden, I will forever yearn for a similarly carefree Heaven.

But if, instead of starting elsewhere, in some erewhon-nowhere of the imagination, I start where I am, what then?

If, instead of looking for impersonal laws, I start with myself, who am I? If, instead of directing my attention to others' self-interest, I consider my own self-assertion, what do I find? What does it mean to be a person?

The first requirement of being a person is being, existence. *Cogito ergo sum, dubito ergo sum*—there are many ways of saying it. But I do not think unless I have something to think about, nor can I doubt unless I have already been credulous. There is, in short, no way of making a standing start; I am always in the midst of life. My life is mine; yet it is presented to me and so is somehow not mine. Both my life and I exist.

Existence requires continuity. Continuity requires identity. I cannot continue in any meaningful sense except as I remain in some way the same. Continuity requires time, and time is not definable unless the present is in some way different from the past.

We may sum up these (and no doubt many other) requirements in the proposition that self-assertion requires self-maintenance. I must maintain my identity through the time of my existence. I must; I am required to do so; I am compelled to do so. This is a special and curious compulsion. It does not come from outside, like a slave driver's whip. Nor does it come from inside, like a neurosis. This compulsion is the same as my existence. The alternative is nonexistence, nonentity, nothingness.

The self that I maintain—the life that I live—is always threatened with dissolution. Only I can forestall that dissolution. If my dissolution is forestalled, I am the one who does it; it is my doing. I can always let myself go—in indolence, drugs, or death: myriads of ways. If I do not let myself go, I hold myself to my life, to the situation in which I have my being—a situation that is extended in space and in time, in society and in history.

Yet of course I am continually letting myself go, because I cannot hold on. The present is inexorably taken away from me. What makes the past past is change in my life. I am plainly in an impossible situation: I must hold on, I must let go, in the end I will be defeated. This impossible situation is, nevertheless, the only one possible, the alternative being nothingness—an extinction so complete that it is not even *my* extinction. That same alternative, moreover, forces on me responsibility for my impossible situation. I am the one who must hold on here and let go there, for I do not exist except in this, my holding on and letting go. I do not exist except in my doing, in my willing and acting.

There is no gainsaying the fact that this program is uncongenial to the modernist temper. People today see themselves in the grip of forces beyond their control. Although C. P. Snow's two cultures fail to understand each other, they tend to agree on their basic irresponsibility. The one is a stranger and afraid, the other a sophisticated servomechanism. These are the fruits of analysis that starts outside of myself. If I am not I at the start of my search for myself, then there is no one searching, and no search and no discovery.

This much may be granted by the modernist outlook; but almost immediately a move is made to shift off the point, and I am asked to listen to stories about how my search is controlled by my id, or how my perceptions are limited by my genes, or how my judgment is affected by the appearance or nonappearance of certain trace elements in my brain cells. All of these stories may well be true, but they are not the point. The point is that these stories do not tell themselves; someone tells them. They do not sound in a silence. If they are meaningful, they are consistent; and if they are consistent, their consistency will include the teller, for without a teller—you, me, or someone—they cannot be told.

Many are tempted to say that consistency is a false or unnecessary or impossible demand. If so, they cannot tell you or me about it, for their telling depends on the physiological regularity of their voice production and our hearing, on the physical regularity of acoustics, on the historical and social usages of their words. Communication demands at least these consistencies; and as Tom Lehrer says, if you can't communicate, the least you can do is shut up.

You may tell stories about my id, genes, and trace elements and thus try to deny my autonomy—and even succeed in doing it. But even then *your* autonomy as a storyteller remains and must remain. You may be able to prove that I am out of my mind, crazy, irresponsible; but you cannot at the same time prove your own irresponsibility, for if you are irresponsible, your proof is not worth attending to. At this point some have claimed that they may be (willy-nilly) telling the truth because they have been programmed to do so. Such alleged meaning can only be an external accident, as a watch with a broken mainspring is correct twice a day. The trouble is that there is no way of knowing when the correct accident occurs and so no way even of identifying its correctness.

The possibility of asserting truth *requires* the possibility of error. The possibility of depending on the reliability of nature requires human fallibility. Galileo was a human being; Newton was a human being; Einstein was a human being. A remarkable thing about these human beings is that we have selected them for our attention, brushing aside other human beings who contended that the earth is flat or that old ladies can fly on broomsticks or what you will. These other human beings were, we say, wrong, and we can give reasons. The human beings we attend to were right, and again we can give reasons. The important thing about their rightness is that it didn't come naturally; they might have made mistakes, and certainly did so on other occasions. In short, the certainty of physics depends upon the possibility of error. Human beings can make mistakes and so can assert truths, including those of physics. Being fallible, human beings cannot be like brass balls rolling down an inclined plane. Ortega said that "Man has no nature, what he has is history."

The foregoing may seem simple and commonsensical and too obvious to bother with. To emphasize its importance, let us boldly say that it is the comprehensive theory of which Einstein's theories, both the general and the special, are instances. Einstein's initial problem was that of synchronizing

two clocks. It turned out that Einstein's task of synchronization could not be performed except by identifying the specific coordinate system of a specific observer (that is, the
performer), who said that in his system, from his point of
view, the clocks were synchronous. In the Newtonian world
of absolute space and time—a coordinate system zeroed by
Copernicus on the sun—the point of view of the observer
was not considered. In effect, he did not exist. But in actuality he (you and I) does exist, and it was Einstein's great
achievement to make his existence and his motion consistent
with the existence of a physical world in motion.

In the same way, we are insisting that the consistency of
every universe of discourse depends on the integral inclu-
sion of the observer, the experimenter, the storyteller. His
autonomy must be part of the system. If there is no autonomous observer—if you and I don't exist—there is no way of
saying that the system exists. There is no saying at all.

In the history of thought it has been the role of God to
proclaim existence. But an all-powerful God allows our apparent autonomy only by His grace and is in no way obli-
gated to us. Similarly, absolute space and time go their
immutable ways without regard to us and our clocks and
telescopes. The thrust of what must be post-modernist
thought is that consistency demands autonomy. Put it the
other way around: No system—no universe of discourse—
that denies autonomy is consistent with its own existence.
This is true of physics and psychology, the systems that
many have tried to substitute for economics, and it is true of
economics itself.

iii

We must not forget how we got here. The fathers of economics told us they were studying the implications of our self-
interest. For our part we concluded that our subject was
rather our self-assertion, and we have found that, even for
the most abstract and recondite sciences, such assertion is an

indispensable point of departure. This assertive self, therefore, is no insignificant thing. It is always with us.

The assertive self is what is generally called the will.
There are three aspects of the will that are especially important for our study of economics: it is embodied; it has a past;
and it has limits.

To say that the will is embodied is merely to say that I am
part of my world. Whatever the world is—matter or energy
or tension or what you will—that I am also. If it were not so,
the consistency we have spoken of would be empty, and our
accounts of the world meaningless. On the most ordinary
level, if I were not part of the world—and the world not part
of me—I could simply let it go, forget about it, pay it no
mind. Of course, my body would then melt, thaw, and resolve itself into a dew, but this disintegration of my body
would not, on the premises, affect me. All who believe this
are welcome to act upon it. Those of us who remain will
conclude that the natural world is not a matter of indifference to us, because our body makes us a part of it and it a
part of us. That we are embodied is constitutional, not acci-
dental.

That the will has a past we have already remarked.
Descartes could not have doubted had he not previously believed. The will is shaped by its past. If you want to be a
physicist, you will have to study calculus. There is no royal
road. If you fail to study calculus, you are closed off—regardless of your propensities and desires—from becoming a
physicist.

This biographical foreclosure is at the same time a historical consequence. The calculus was once unnecessary—un-
heard of—for physical experiment. Franklin, who was
twenty-one when Newton died, was no mathematician; yet
he made important discoveries. Not only does history control the possibility of solving problems, it also dictates the
problems to be solved. The problems Copernicus faced were
those left by Ptolemy; there would have been no Einstein
had there been no Newton. To take an example from political economy, the notion of an oil-depletion allowance could

not have occurred to anyone before Edwin L. Drake drilled his first well in 1859, or before the income-tax amendment was adopted in 1913. Similar examples can be cited concerning the most elemental goods: wheat was of small account in the Orient until recently; and the price of wheat yesterday is a factor in the price of wheat today.

The limitation of my will follows from its existence. Whatever exists can be defined. Whatever is defined is this, *not* that. I am *not* you. Because you are thus essential to my definition, you are, in the most fundamental sense, essential to me. If I destroy you, I destroy part of myself. My existence may require your destruction, as in war; but whenever and however I wrong you, I diminish myself. This is the ethical sanction; there is no other.

My autonomy requires this sanction. It is not imposed on me but is flesh of my flesh and bone of my bone. In detail it may be concerned with my superego, with encapsulated love for or fear of my parents, or with what I learned before (or after) the age of seven. But in principle, and regardless of the details, it is an aspect of the compulsion that I maintain my existence.

As a consequence of the compulsion to maintain my existence, I must maintain yours; and on this requirement economics is grounded. Economics is not a question of an alleged propensity to barter or to seek profit, nor is it a question of the properties of numbers. Economics is a question of the relations of human beings with one another.

Economic relations are special relations in that they are all concerned with money. Money is the distinguishing idea of economics. Without money, all the other economic ideas either do not appear (price) or fall back into general ethics (rights) or general psychology (demand) or general physiology (consumption) or agriculture and engineering (production).

To money, therefore, we now direct our attention.

5

MONEY

The Distinguishing Mark of Economics

i

According to tradition, money was invented in Lydia, a small kingdom in western Asia Minor, in the seventh century B.C. Before that time and place many of the uses of money were served in various ways, but money itself did not exist. It was unknown to the heroes of whom Homer sang. There is little mention of it in the Old Testament. Yet without money our present civilization could not exist, could not have come into existence. As we cannot escape history, we cannot escape money.

David Hume and many others have written that money is a convenience: "'Tis the oil, which renders the motion of the wheels more smooth and easy." But it is more than that, and different from that. It is not a convenience or a tool. A hammer is a tool; it is useful—arguably necessary—in building a building, but the finished structure—even the partially finished structure—can be, and is, described and defined without reference to hammers used in construction. A yardstick, however, is different. Measuring is essential not only in the construction of the building but in the description of the size of the whole and of the parts, and of the relation of part to part. Without measuring, the structure is formless, and a description of it is merely a list of building materials and their sense qualities. Measuring is similarly necessary and creative in economic affairs, and economic measuring is done with money.

In general, measuring is a comparing of something with some standard. For example, by laying a ruler across this book, you determine that the page is about 5½ inches wide. But how long is an inch? Well, an inch is ⅟₃₆ of a yard, and since 1893 a yard has been 3600/3973 of a meter. Originally, as one of the reforms of the French Revolution, a meter was defined as 1/1000 of a kilometer, which in turn was 1/10000 of the surface distance from the equator to either pole. Of course that distance could not be measured directly, especially not by laying a meter stick along the route ten million times (that would be a literally circular fallacy). Instead, reliance was put on geometry, which gave the circumference of the earth as $2\pi r$, and the distance from the pole to the equator as $2\pi r/4$. The radius of the earth is stated in terms of some unit of measurement. When it was first calculated with reasonable accuracy, by Eratosthenes in the third century B.C., the unit was the stadium, which may have been equal to 600 of some king's feet. In Newton's time, and in the time of the French Revolution, the unit was the yard, which may have been the length of some king's stride. So we have come full circle after all: a yard is defined in terms of a meter, and a meter is defined in terms of a yard.

In the meantime, frequent refinements in measuring the radius of the earth led to unsettling changes in the length of a meter. Consequently it was agreed that a meter was the distance between two scratches on a certain platinum-iridium bar. This bar, which was deposited in Sèvres, outside of Paris, was obviously more precise than the meter stick incised on a slab of marble that in 1848 was built into the wall of the Chancellery (now the Ministry of Justice) in the Place Vendôme in Paris, where it can still be seen. But both meter sticks—the marble one and the platinum-iridium one—were perfectly arbitrary. The present standard, in use since 1960, which is equal to 1,650,763.73 wavelengths of the red-orange light given off by krypton-86, is more convenient since it can be used by scientists everywhere (provided they have the right instruments), but it is no less arbitrary. In the end, as it was in the beginning, we stand up and declare that *this* is a meter, and no fooling. We are back to self-assertion.

There are two further points to be made about measuring. First, the relationship between the measuring standard and the thing measured is not reciprocal. This book is about 5½ inches wide; but an inch is not defined as 2/11 of the width of this book. The standard defines the thing, not vice versa; the alternative is circular reasoning of the sort that developed at the start of the metric system. This point is sadly often overlooked by economists.

Second, the meter standard, though perfectly arbitrary and, moreover, consciously agreed upon, is not a convention in the sense that a red light means danger or stop or the port side of a ship, or that a tennis set, which used to have to be won by two games, can now be settled by a tie breaker. The nautical rules of the road, which are conventional, require ships meeting head on to pass red to red, that is, left side to left side; and everyone, with the exception of the British and some others, has adopted the same system for highways. It is convenient to have an agreed-on system; but it would not be impossible for drivers of cars meeting each other to get out and debate the right of way, as I have seen happen on a narrow road in Greece. Without the rules of the road, no one has the right of way, but the right of way implies nothing beyond itself. Using a yardstick, on the other hand, defines spatial relations, and hence space. Space is an inevitability, not a convenience. A game, of course, is not even a convenience. The introduction of the tie breaker changed the strategy of tennis, but this matters only to tennis players, and no one has to be a tennis player. One can't help being spatially oriented, and the orientation had better be measurable. If not, the physical universe is beyond comprehension, and ordinary life chancy.

ii

The ancients were casual about weights and measures. The cubit was the distance from one's elbow to the tip of one's middle finger. Obviously this changed from person to person, and even in the same person from time to time. Limited attempts at standardization were made then (or have since been made by scholars), so that it is said that the ancient Egyptian cubit was 52.5 cm., while the Greek was 46.29 cm., the Hebrew 44.65 cm., and the Roman 44.36 cm. Measurement of time was even more vagrant, since everywhere except in Egypt the time from sunrise to sunset was divided into twelve hours, and likewise the time from sunset to sunrise, the length of an hour thus varying from day to night, from season to season, and from latitude to latitude. The Western world consequently had no reliable clock until the fourteenth century, and even two hundred years later so much ingenuity was invested in making clocks that showed the phases of the moon and the like that fine measurement was disregarded and Galileo had trouble timing his first experiments.

In any event there was little need for universal systems of measurement until the rise of experimental science. So long as the world was a parade of miracles and portents, measurement played no role in understanding, and replication of awesome events was unthinkable. Precision was, to be sure, required in building, and it was readily attained: foundations were level, the proportion of part to part was meticulously observed, and stones were fitted one to another so closely that a knife could not be slipped between them. Such precision, however, did not need to be universal; it merely needed to be consistent within the bounds of each separate building. Whatever the cubit used in the construction of the Parthenon, it was strictly followed, but a different unit could have been used for the Odeon of Herodes Atticus, a stone's throw away. In the same way it was, within the memory of men now living, not unusual for New England farmers to erect barns using not a yardstick but a "story pole," various multiples of which yielded the desired proportions. I myself have used a story pole and found it handy in building a trued and squared playroom in a roughly finished cellar.

Local systems of measurement are satisfactory for local purposes and can even be pressed into the service of specific large projects such as Newton's (in any case, astronomy had long had one important universal system of measuring—that of measuring angles). Though the scientific revolution had started in the sixteenth century, it was not until after the invention of the metric system that the remarkable burgeoning of physical science began. In the same way, trade requires stable and changeless measuring units, and the spread of such units calls trade into existence. The Lydian invention, which was quickly and widely embraced in the Mediterranean world, made possible the slow, halting, and still continuing shift away from a world of plunder and rapine.

The facts that trade grew so slowly, that almost every jurisdiction boasted its own currency, that statistical information was almost nonexistent, and that for two and a half millennia the only money that men were conscious of was coined money—these facts for a long time hid the further fact that though both a yardstick and a dollar are measuring units, they measure in fundamentally different ways.

iii

When we were buying our present house I made some measurements, using a steel tape I've since lost, and determined that the room I'm now writing in was eleven feet two inches by sixteen feet seven inches. That was almost twenty-five years ago. This morning I measured the room again, using a wooden (presumably birch) yardstick given me by the local hardware store. The answer this morning was the same as that a quarter century ago: eleven two by sixteen seven.

Now, when we bought the house all those years ago we paid a certain number of dollars for it. Of course, we gave the seller a certified check, but we could have legally tendered him a stack of dollar bills. If we were to sell the house today, we'd receive from the buyer a certified check, but the number of dollars represented by the check would (I trust) be considerably larger than what we paid. If the buyer tendered us a stack of dollar bills, they'd look almost the same as those of twenty-five years ago, but it would take many more of them to accomplish the same purpose. The house would be substantially the same, but the price would be different. On the record it's hard to avoid concluding that the measuring unit has changed.

Nothing like this happens with physical measuring units. The steel tape I lost expanded or contracted a bit as the weather was warmer or colder, but this change could, if necessary, be allowed for, or the temperature controlled. If a thermometer is calibrated so that the freezing point for water at sea level is 32 degrees and the boiling point 212 degrees, then the normal temperature of the human body will be 98.6 degrees today, tomorrow, next year, or next century. If the boiling point is taken as 100 degrees and the freezing point 0 degrees, it is easy to make the appropriate conversions from Fahrenheit to Celsius. Without this uniformity, chemistry would be impossible or at least greatly reduced in power. A talented cook can achieve brilliant results by seasoning to taste; but if you want to get water from hydrogen and oxygen, your proportions have to be precise, and precise proportions always give you the same result.

It is clear that a dollar does not measure physical properties of objects, nor does a yardstick measure economic properties. Nowhere is there a standard for the franc or the dollar similar to the platinum-iridium bar at Sèvres. Even when the dollar was said to be redeemable for 15 $\frac{5}{21}$ grains of gold $\frac{9}{10}$ fine, there was no need for—indeed no possibility of—comparing a dollar bill with a lump (very small) of such gold. Furthermore, a mason can lay his meter stick against a stone he wants to measure and immediately have his answer, but there is no point to laying a dollar bill alongside something one wants to buy. A physical measurement is direct and absolute, but a monetary measurement is somehow different.

The difference is hinted at by Plato and even more explicitly by Aristotle. In the *Republic* Socrates asks, "How will [merchants] exchange their productions?" Plato's brother Adeimantes replies, "Clearly they will buy and sell." Whereupon Socrates concludes, "Then they will need a market-place, and a token for purposes of exchange." Whatever Plato may have meant by "token" (*symbolon*), he plainly meant something more than physical. In the *Nichomachean Ethics* Aristotle puts it this way: "All things that are exchanged must be somehow comparable. It is for this end that money has been introduced, and it becomes in a sense an intermediate; for it measures all things . . . how many shoes are equal to a house or a given amount of food."

"In a sense an intermediate." In the Newtonian world, a meter stick is immediate in its application. But in the economic world money is intermediate. The measurements of this room are in a one-to-one relation with a measuring stick. But the dollar value of this house establishes an indirect relationship with the dollar value of shoes—and ships and sealing wax.

Unlike shoes and other goods, money is ambiguous in its meaning. The dollar bill I have in my pocket is an asset to me, but represents a debt of the nation. The balance in my checking account is also an asset to me, but it is a liability to the bank. On the other hand, the check I put in the mail to my creditor will be an asset to him but a debit to me. In contrast, goods are goods to whoever holds them, and are nothing to anybody else, except as they enter into and so swell the national commerce.

Another ambiguity of money was revealed by Keynes's analysis of what he called "liquidity preference," which is partly a function of the convenience of keeping money at hand for the transaction of ordinary business, and partly a function of holding money as a store of wealth because of uncertainty about the trend of the economy. A strong preference for liquidity thus indicates grave doubts about future business, and at the same time great faith in the continuing strength of the money-issuing institution, which strength must in turn be based on the state of business.

These ambiguities confirm Aristotle's description of money as an intermediary, which looks both ways.

iv

We should not be surprised to have discovered that economics and Newtonian physics, which are fundamentally different, should have fundamentally different ways of measuring.

It is nevertheless disturbing to find money floating, as it were, between goods, instead of setting an unequivocal value on each one; and this idea (which Plato and Aristotle did not develop beyond the hints we have quoted) has been resisted, and is resisted to this day.

The resistance has taken several forms, including the search for some rare and durable commodity (usually gold or silver) to act in the same way as physical measurement, the quantity theory of money (now available in old and new versions), and the attempt to devise a "constant dollar" through the creation of indices of one sort or another.

The trouble with the first notion is that money has never been merely a rare and durable commodity. Even when such a commodity has been the money of account, the work of money has also been done in other ways. A society in which the only acknowledged money is gold, and in which fractional-reserve banking is unknown or prohibited, will still do much—perhaps most—of its business on credit. Small retail transactions may be carried out with cash on the barrel head, but any work done for hire—to take the simplest case—involves credit. Either the work is paid for in advance, in which case the hirer is extending credit to the hired, or, in the more usual case, the hired extends credit by doing the work first and being paid weekly or monthly or when the job is done. There is, in fact, no other way of doing such business; if the pay were measured out as the work proceeded, both the hired and the hirer would be so preoccupied that neither would be able to get any work done.

This credit relationship does not, of course, increase the number of gold coins circulating in the economy. If in my business the application of a hundred dollars' worth of labor to a hundred dollars' worth of raw materials will produce something I can sell for three hundred dollars, I need only a hundred dollars to get things rolling. I use my money—all hard coin carefully counted out—to buy the raw materials. When my employees have done their work, I take the finished product and sell it for the three hundred dollars, again hard coin, a hundred dollars of which I pay my employees, leaving me with my original hundred dollars plus a hundred dollars' profit. Putting the profit aside for consideration in another chapter, we see that my implicit credit arrangement with my employees, together with my skill or luck in selling the product quickly (or in advance), made it possible for my hundred dollars to underwrite the work of several hundred dollars. Everything was paid for in hard coin; not even fully convertible paper money was used. There were no substitutes offered or accepted. Credit multiplied the use of that hard coin and made work for my employees, a profit for me, and goods for the purchaser.

There are two important lessons to be learned from this little scenario. The first is that money is not merely a method of measuring a static situation but is essential for planning and contracting ahead. The employees and I could agree on the work and the pay because money enabled us to compare the value to each of us of their present work and their future pay. As a yardstick measures and thus defines a static situation, money measures and thus defines a dynamic situation, one in which people reach present agreement for future action. Without money, the employment relationship is at best share cropping and at worst slavery.

The second important lesson is that money is not a sterile object. The physical quantity of it that you have, or that the nation has, is almost the least significant thing about it. If this is true of hard coin, it is obviously also true of paper money. The distinction that is popularly made between them breaks down because both are expanded in the same way by credit.

The world we actually live in is of course far more sophisticated in the explicit use of credit than is the world of our scenario. Besides the credit implicit in all the payrolls of all the industries, the explicit instruments, from credit cards and mortgages to demand notes and long-term bonds, greatly expand the effectiveness of money. Because of such credit, there is a bit of a banker in all of us.

The banking system creates money by lending more than it takes in. Either the law or the action of the bank's directors determines the reserve it will maintain. If the reserve is 20 percent (which would be high), the bank will receive my deposit of $100, credit my account with that amount, and lend you $80, which you can deposit in your bank. Your bank will credit you with the $80 and lend your neighbor $64, and this process may be continued (always using a different bank) until my $100 has become (subject to some friction) $500 at work in the economy.

It cannot be too frequently and too strongly emphasized that, just like the employees' credit, fractional-reserve banking can proceed even if the government deals only in gold coins. Today most business goes on with the use of checks, and as electronic systems are developed, more and more of it will be done by my bank's computer talking to your bank's, but the principle is the same.

v

The basic problem for a quantity theory of money is obviously that of determining the quantity. If you want to know how much money you have, how do you set about counting it? You can count your spoons and arrive at a precise number that will satisfy even an analytical philosopher. Bertrand Russell writes that "if a set of numbers can be used as names of a set of objects, each number occurring only once, the number of numbers used as names is the same as the number of objects." This may seem like an odd procedure, but you can certainly follow it with your spoons and will then know how many people (presumably counting them the same way) you can invite to dinner.

Even when you seem to do that with the cash in your pocket, it would appear that the folding money is a different sort of object from the coin. The number of greenbacks you have is less significant than the figures engraved on each one. Still more esoteric and insubstantial is the money in your checking account, which can nevertheless be added to and subtracted from and thus counted. But there's more to it than that. You may have some stocks and bonds, perhaps all of them listed on the New York Stock Exchange and so sufficiently liquid for you to sell them at a moment's notice; the money you can get for them varies from moment to moment. Others of your holdings are probably less liquid. If you have a house for sale, it will certainly take you weeks, and may take you months, to find a buyer willing to pay you almost what you hope it's worth. What you might get for your books and furniture is even more chancy.

Your stocks and bonds and house and chattels are counted as part of your wealth but not part of your money. This seems a distinction without a difference, because your credit depends in part on your wealth. For most of us, with comparatively little net wealth, our credit depends on our income. In either case, we can spend our credit like ordinary money—and more easily than ordinary money, a credit card being more convenient to handle than a pocketful of change. The total credit we have is not fixed, and it depends upon our continuing sources of income, that is, upon us as going concerns.

This imprecision is compounded when attempts are made to determine the national money supply. To try to meet the problem, economists define money in several different ways and make estimates of the amounts of each, pronouncing that one kind of money is more significant in one situation than in others. Accordingly M-1 consists of currency, traveler's checks, and checking deposits (M-1A includes only checking deposits in commercial banks, while M-1B also includes NOW accounts and deposits against which checks can be drawn in savings and loan associations and certain other institutions). M-2 adds in ordinary savings and time deposits, money-market funds, and overnight Eurodollar deposits, but it does not count time deposits of $100,000 or more. M-3 has no $100,000 limitation and also counts repurchase agreements. In January 1983 the Federal Reserve Board announced the following totals: M-1, $482.1 billion; M-2, $2,010.0 billion; and M-3, $2,403.3 billion. There are reasons, which need not detain us, for these various definitions and widely various totals. We merely note that their very variety indicates that the money supply the Federal Reserve Board claims it regulates is not an unequivocal quantity.

Of course it is not necessary to know exactly what the money supply is before acting to increase or decrease it. Nor is it necessary to do the increasing or decreasing in any particular way. There are in fact several ways, but none of them satisfies the popular imagination of running the printing presses faster or slower. What is actually done is to make it easier or more difficult for banks to make loans, which makes it easier or more difficult for businesses and individuals to borrow money. The amount of credit in the economy, and consequently the amount of money, is thus increased or decreased.

The increase or decrease, however, is not automatic, though many seem to think it is. As noted, our individual credit depends largely on our income; for obvious reasons, banks are not eager to lend money to the unemployed. Businesses, too, must be going concerns if they expect to expand their credit. In a stagnant economy it is difficult to expand the money supply because few want to be borrowers or lenders. Businesses are leery of producing what they cannot sell, and banks are leery of lending to somnolent businesses.

vi

Quantity theorists are not daunted by the vagueness of their basic number but feed it into an equation that says that the quantity of money, multiplied by the velocity of its circulation, is equal to the general price level, multiplied by the goods produced. The equation, written all in capitals, looks formidable ($MV = PY$) but expresses a simple, even a simplistic, idea.

Difficulties occur with each term. We have already seen that M is seldom what it seems. Next, it turns out that velocity (V) cannot be determined except by means of this equation. Fanciers of the quantity theory contend that over the past many years V has been fairly constant; so MV is practically a single term.

The right-hand side of the equation presents different difficulties. Y represents the total of the goods and services produced, that is, the real (stated in things), as opposed to the nominal (stated in money), gross national product. In a later chapter, we will contend that the GNP, whether real or nominal, is less than it's cracked up to be, but for the moment we will accept it at its face value. We are immediately struck by the fact that its face value is expressed in money, that is, nominally. Moreover, it cannot be expressed in any other way, for money is the only unit of measurement applicable to apples and pears and tons of steel and all the rest. The paradoxical fact is that the "real" GNP can only be quantified "nominally."

What then is the price level (P)? It is an index, such as we will discuss in a later section, derived by combining the prices of a great variety of goods and services, each one weighted to allow it its proper importance in the economy. But of course the prices of the goods and services are already and necessarily included in the GNP, which cannot otherwise be added up. So the only way that multiplying the price level by the GNP could make any sense would be for the GNP to be expressed somehow other than in money. And that we have seen to be impossible. For this reason, many monetarists have dropped P from the right-hand side of the equation and talk only of output (Y). Thus the new quantity theory of money is $MV = Y$.

Since MV is, after all, a single term arbitrarily split according to the definition of M that one uses, the monetarist equation comes down to this: The total money spent for goods and services equals the total prices of those goods and services. That, in a word, is a tautology, but on it is based the monetarist policy recommendation that the money supply be increased steadily at an annual rate of, say, 4 percent, thus producing a 4 percent annual increase in output. This seems plausible until one wonders, Why not 100 percent? Or 10,000 percent? If prosperity is that easy, why be so restrained? God knows we could stand a few good times.

*

vii

Of course, everyone knows the consequences of expanding the money supply without restraint. Even though the formula for the quantity of money doesn't reveal the consequences, the question is haunted by the runaway inflation of the Weimar Republic in the early 1920s. Everyone has heard the tales of wheelbarrowfuls of marks for a loaf of bread; and folk wisdom is convinced that the hyperinflation ruined the German middle class (whose savings vanished as the marks rolled from the presses), destroyed the national morale, and so brought on Hitler and World War II and the rise of the Soviet Union and the threat of nuclear holocaust.

What actually happened, however, is quite different, and very much to our present point. The center did not hold, because it had already been destroyed. First, there was not much of a German middle class to begin with. What there was made its first appearance on the stage of history, not as independent farmers and small entrepreneurs, as in the United States, but as the bureaucracy of the multitudinous German states, whose alleged spirit of public service was important in Hegel's theory of the state. By the middle of the nineteenth century, it was possible for Marx, writing voluminously about the bourgeoisie, to have in mind a ruling class, not a middle class, and to foresee the progressive narrowing of that class as its weaker members dropped, or were forced, down into the proletariat. Imperial Germany, on the eve of World War I, was very much the creature of the old nobility, the landed Junkers, and a handful of large, cartel-oriented industrialists, who were themselves often of the nobility.

Second, such middle class as there was suffered the primary erosion of its position during the war, not afterward. Hjalmar Schacht, no wild-eyed radical, wrote that during the war there was a "bountiful flow of money from the coffers of the Treasury into the pockets of the [industrialists and Junker agriculturalists]" and contrasted this policy with the relatively heavy wartime taxation in the United Kingdom and the United States. At the other end, he pointed out that the ratio of middle management wages to those of unskilled labor fell from 347:100 in 1913 to 147:100 in 1922.

Third, though Germany was the land of Kant and Beethoven and Goethe, it was also the land of dueling scars and glorified violence. Every attempt to stabilize society—let alone to observe the peace treaty—was met by slander in the press and murder in the streets. Foreign Minister Walther Rathenau, butt of Nationalist anti-Semitic attacks from 1918 on, who was murdered in 1922, was only the most prominent of literally thousands of victims.

Finally, the German talent for abstract theorizing had found outlet in the proportional representation provisions of the Weimar constitution. As a result the electorate was fragmented, and everyone was encouraged to vote his prejudices and his pocketbook. The creation of a coalition capable of governing was rendered almost impossible.

All of this had happened before the printing presses started to roll out the marks. In *The Economic Consequences of the Peace*, written in 1919, Keynes cited a remark attributed to Lenin to the effect that "the best way to destroy the Capitalist System was to debauch the currency." And he warned that German prices, then running at five times those of 1913, would have to go to fifteen or twenty times because of the provisions of the peace treaty. All this was very bad; but that it was not necessarily disastrous is indicated by the fact that France was then in a similar situation, as is Israel today. The point is that hyperinflation followed in Germany because the society had already been compromised to the verge of destruction. Germany was not a going concern, and for this reason its currency became worthless. All the schemes for basing the mark on rye or coal or kilowatts or whatever failed, because commodities, like money, are valuable only in a going concern.

*

viii

A third attempt to escape the meaning of the intermediate role of money takes the form of constructing indices of consumer prices, wholesale prices, and so on.

People speak of the purchasing power of money and call attention to the declining value of the dollar. These ways of speaking seem to assume that money has value, like any good or service, and that this value can be measured. Measuring the value of the dollar would mean comparing it with something else, either the "market basket" of the Consumer Price Index or something similar. Though the contents of the market basket can be changed by legislative or executive or merely professional fiat, the basket seems real, while money seems only nominal, or as Marx called it, a "purely ideal or mental" form of value. But measurement, as we have seen, is not reciprocal; so if the value of money is stated in terms of a market basket, the basket becomes the standard of measurement, and money becomes a commodity with a curiously elevated price.

There is no objection in principle to making this market basket, or any part of it, or anything else, our unit of account. As everyone who has had a little Latin or Anglo-Saxon knows, many ancient peoples counted their wealth in terms of cattle, as the Masai do today. This is clumsy and imprecise, but not impossible. But if we did something like this, we should not delude ourselves—as I fear our econometricians do—into thinking we had established a "constant dollar."

No market basket is the same to different people at any given time (my wife and I set up housekeeping a number of years ago; so we are now relatively unconcerned with the price of furniture). Nor is the basket the same in different historical situations. Of all the things in the basket, the price of bread is sometimes urged as basic, and it was indeed a central issue in the French Revolution. But today food is so small a part of the family budget, and bread so indifferent a part of the diet, that all the bakeries in the land could shut down tomorrow without causing even much inconvenience, let alone starvation. It is the same with indices of industrial prices: the price of steel is of much less importance to a book publisher than it is to a builder of office buildings; and it is more to a builder today than it was before the inventions of the elevator and the electric light made skyscrapers possible.

The constructors of indices are of course not unaware of such shifts of demand, and they try to keep up with them by shifting and refining the contents of their market baskets. Such shifting obviously compromises the constancy of the index, which thus becomes a historical standard, like any other form of money. Indexing—like so many other things economists have done from Adam Smith onward—is an attempt to escape history and to reduce economics to an automatic happening. It is also in direct conflict with the system it pretends to serve. Conventional economics says that a market economy, through constant shifts in relative prices of goods and services, is the most efficient way of allocating limited resources. But the whole end and purpose of all the attempts to measure with "constant dollars" is to nullify market price shifts. If all prices went up (or down) in precise lockstep, there would be no need to try to freeze them with an index. The inflation that everyone deplores is not all prices going up together; it is some going up much faster than others, to the delight of some people and countries, and to the dismay, or even distress, of others.

A major reason why prices do not go up or down in lockstep is that different businesses require different lengths of time to produce their goods. Consequently the contracts they enter into with their suppliers are for different lengths of time, requiring both parties to estimate prices months or even years ahead. If inflation is proceeding erratically, many such estimates will prove disastrously wrong. But if the inflationary path is relatively smooth, even though steep, most businesses can adjust as well to high inflation as to none. Thus in the United States, the inflationary rate of 1983 and 1984 was no great obstacle to the so-called recovery, even though the rate was many times that of the early postwar years when inflation first became a political issue.

ix

In the extreme case, indexing is far from harmless. The reason is appropriately given in a 1923 lament of Hans von Raumer, minister of economics in the Weimar Republic. "The root of the evil," von Raumer said, "is the depreciation adjustment [that is, the index]. Inflation goes on unchecked because one must add enormous increments onto wages and prices alike, and these in their turn work in such a manner that the depreciation provided for actually occurs through the inflation thus caused."

It should be emphasized that the attempt to devise a constant dollar is launched in the hope that the economic world can thereby be placed beyond the reach of human judgment and the errors and vices to which it is prone. But it is not so easy to escape the necessity for judgment. Indexing, in fact, depends on judgment from the very beginning, for someone (or a committee of someones) must decide which items are to be included and how the various items are to be weighted. And someone must decide how the weighting is to be changed from time to time. In 1982 a considerable shift in the Consumer Price Index was caused by a shift in the weighting of the mortgage rate as a factor in the cost of housing. "Someone must decide." We are back to self-assertion.

x

If we now look back at what Bertrand Russell said about counting, we will see that there is no "realistic" way of counting either our personal money or our national money. The reason, of course, is that our money is not real in the sense that our spoons are real. Our money is our credit; our national money is our "full faith and credit," as is said on government bonds.

As a practical matter, it is well understood that money depends on faith, that it passes from hand to hand because people have faith that it is what it purports to be. When the king of Lydia put his stamp on a lump of electrum, traders all over the Mediterranean had faith that the lump weighed what the stamp said. It was no longer necessary for traders to carry scales and weights with them at all times—as was done until recently on the Gold Coast—and make an elaborate ritual of the simplest transaction. Buying and selling could be accomplished in the few minutes it took to count out and examine the necessary coins. The velocity of money improved.

Clipping and counterfeiting of course became worrisome, and various ways of combatting them were developed. One of the most remarkable was devised by thirteenth-century Florence, where it became customary to circulate brand-new florins in small leather bags sealed by the mint. It is noticeable that acceptance of these purses was still an act of faith; it was assumed that they contained genuine and sound florins because one had faith in the inviolability of the purse and the legitimacy of the seal.

What may be insufficiently noticed is that faith in money neither starts nor ends with the currency itself. Obviously something more than appreciation of the design or printing is at work in the acceptance of inconvertible paper money. It is made legal tender by law or acceptable by custom. It, too, can be counterfeited and so circulates only on faith in its genuineness; to this extent it is like coin. In the same way, checks can be forged or kited, and balances can be overdrawn, and banks can fail.

The more fundamental and fruitful faith is in the society as a going concern. What is at stake is not the purity or genuineness of the money per se, but confidence in the continuity of a society in which money can be spent. The South will not rise again; so Confederate money is of value only to collectors, and Confederate war debts (and thus war credits) were wiped out by the Fourteenth Amendment.

An unstated reason for the persisting interest in gold—in "hard money" generally—is an aloofness from the present polity. This is more than liquidity preference, but expresses a willingness to opt out of the present society and an expectation of maintaining one's position in a successor commonwealth. This, too, is an act of faith, and one not infrequently belied by the event. Hoards invite plunder or confiscation. The Inca's treasure did him no good.

Nor does faith in money stop with faith in a society in which money may be spent. What matters at least as much is that the society will be such that what is bought with money may be peaceably used and enjoyed. Society is a going concern.

Thus the acceptance and circulation of money is possible only when we have faith in our fellows and in the society created with them. This faith is active; it is shown in what we do, and nowhere else. Faith is self-assertion again. What we do shows the sort of people we are and the sort of society we will have. "What sort of people do they think we are?" Churchill asked scornfully as he took command of the war against the Nazis. In economics, the sort of society we will have is shown by the sorts of exchanges we make among ourselves. This will be our next subject.

6

EXCHANGE

How Economic Activity Civilizes

i

In the ancient world justice was a reciprocal relationship between individuals, and so was trade. Aristotle cites the Pythagoreans as recommending literal reciprocity, a theory which with the Jews was the Mosaic talion law—an eye for an eye and a tooth for a tooth. After giving reasons for rejecting such literalness, Aristotle writes: "It is by proportionate requital that the city holds together. Men seek to return either evil for evil—and if they cannot do so, think their position mere slavery—or good for good—and if they cannot do so there is no exchange, but it is by exchange that they hold together. That is why they give a prominent place to the temple of the Graces—to promote the requital of services; for this is characteristic of grace—we should serve in return one who has shown grace to us, and should another time take the initiative in showing it."

Aristotle evidently understood grace to be more than prudence or calculation. In the *Republic* Plato had shown, as Adam Smith was to show two millennia later, that the division of labor increases production, and that as a practical matter it makes a just society necessary. But Aristotle had his eye out for what holds the polis together, and what he saw was a system of mutual obligations freely entered into and objectified in exchanges of goods and services.

63

If exchange is thus a factor in justice and in grace, the form of exchange will be a factor in the form of personality. An unjust exchange will be the mark of an unjust person. A personality forming itself in irrational exchange will be to that extent irrational. Thus Odysseus, wise and wily though he is, understands only plunder and the exchange of gifts. The rules by which he lives are arbitrary and enforceable only by the sword or bow and arrow, and his weapons are never far from his hand. The behavior of feudal lords was also unpredictable. Likewise, the Tlingit potlatch may, as the anthropologists say, have served the purpose of redistributing tribal wealth, as well as encouraging achievers to achieve, but it was a remarkably irrational way of doing it, and the chiefs were narrowly honor-ridden men, though often generous and gracious.

The rational is the general or universal. Barter must be an *ad hoc* transaction, but money makes general exchange possible. In *History in Geographic Perspective*, Edward W. Fox shows how maritime or riverine cities (especially in eighteenth-century France, but also in ancient Greece, Tudor England, and elsewhere) were more open, dynamic, and accomplished in self-government than inland cities, whose exchanges reached out only a day's wagon trip from the city walls. John K. Fairbank calls attention to the vigor and progressiveness of the maritime Chinese in contrast to the extreme traditionalism of the "agrarian-bureaucratic empire" at the middle of the Middle Kingdom. Exchange makes for civility, and so for civilization.

Without a modicum of trust, even the simplest barter is impossible. Among barbarians the trust may be minimal: that is what marks them as uncivilized. Yet the most suspicious traders, exchanging a bushel of wheat for a pound of meat, can carry their skeptical examinations only so far. Volume and weight can be readily tested, but it is a nuisance to guard against adulteration. The grains of wheat cannot all be miscroscopically examined, nor the meat be completely dissected, especially if the traders are to do anything else with their time. And anyhow the proof of the foods is in the eating—which must await the consummation of the trade. So if the traders are to do business, they must trust that there are limits to the deviousness of their trading partners. The greater the trust, the easier the trading; the easier the trading, the more trading can be done in a given period of time.

Practically all business depends on the reliable nosiness of the Bureau of Weights and Measures. The meat industry would go out of its mind if it could not base its pricing on USDA standards and regulations. Clamdiggers may grumble, but without regulation they'd dig themselves out of business in short order. Even the stock exchanges provide a dramatic example of the effectiveness of regulation in promoting trade. In the Great Bull Market of blessed memory, the New York Stock Exchange, "self-regulated" as it was, traded roughly four million shares a day (and only 16,410,000 shares were traded in the frenzy of Black Tuesday). It took a long time for people to get over the Depression, but partly because of the interference of the SEC, trading is now at a hundred-million-shares-a-day clip. It is still possible for us to lose our shirts on Wall Street, but it's no longer likely we'll be cheated out of them; so we're more willing to risk them—to our broker's profit, and possibly even to our own.

It is a notable fact that business executives—with one side of their brains—understand all this very well. This is why they spend millions to establish brand names, which are a sort of pledge of product quality. Their reasonable expectation is that weary travelers, unable to face the uncertainty of the local inspection of accommodations, will settle for an interchangeable HoJoMoLo even though they might prefer at least some variety in their plastic decorations. A recent Holiday Inn advertising campaign labored precisely this point. The purpose of brand recognition is to instill consumer confidence and so increase trade.

ii

In near-subsistence societies, where goods are few, exchanges also are few and seldom urgent. Today in Third World countries rural markets are colorful but somnolent.

Rarely can enough be offered for sale to repay much effort, nor is there enough variety to excite potential buyers. Occasionally a spirited haggle will erupt, more as a sociable than as a mercantile event. In such an environment, value tends to be found more in the thought controlling the exchange than in the goods exchanged. Sometimes the controlling thought seems to be a certain rude satisfaction in besting one's trading partner. In happier situations, the traditions of gift giving persist, and exchanges are judged partly on the capabilities and resources of the exchangers. The poor will be treated leniently, as the widow's mites were especially praiseworthy because "she of her want did cast in all that she had, even all her living."

In more prosperous societies, the proper valuation of goods and services becomes an issue. Thus the Church Fathers, whose precepts were based on the equality of all men before the Lord's throne, developed the idea of the just price. "Therefore," St. Thomas argued, "if either the price exceed the quantity of the thing's worth, or, conversely, the thing exceed the price, there is no longer the equality of justice; and consequently to sell a thing for more than its worth, or to buy it for less than its worth, is in itself unjust and unlawful." He saw, however, as his mentor Aristotle had seen before him on the question of justice in general, that this admirable rule was not altogether easy to apply. Among exceptions, he cited "for instance, when a man has great need of a certain thing, while another will suffer if he be without it. In such a case the just price will depend not only on the thing sold, but on the loss which the sale brings on the seller. And thus it will be lawful to sell a thing for more than it is worth in itself, though the price paid be not more than it is worth to the owner." Putting aside the question of what a thing is "worth in itself," we are still left with the implication that trade will be typically conducted in parochial face-to-face exchanges, for only thus will buyer and seller approach the ability to judge each other's needs and potential sufferings. Even then, Aquinas adds, it "depends on a kind of estimate."

The Church's rules, exceptions and all, became meaningless when Venetian merchants sold glassware in Beirut
and bought spices for resale at home. The Venetians certainly got much more for their Murano goblets than they
could have done at home, while the Levantines are likely to
have held up their end. Yet all parties could gain from trade
of this generality; it would be hard to say who suffered from
it.

iii

We have heard Socrates explain to Plato's brother that the
Republic would need a market place. For millennia the market place—agora, forum—was a center of community life.
When civil activity picked up again after the Dark Ages, one
of the signs of rebirth was the growth of fairs. Some markets
of the traditional sort still function in less-developed lands;
and major cities everywhere have fish markets and produce
markets to supply retailers and restaurants. Yet most of us
seldom or never have anything directly to do with these.
When we say we're going to the market, we usually mean a
supermarket, one of a chain, whose operation and structure
are quite different from those of the traditional market.

The traditional market has many sellers of largely interchangeable goods whose production presents no great barrier to new suppliers who want to enter the business. In
such a market there is what is called perfect competition,
and everyone should know that perfection is not for this
world. In a spectrum stretching to the right of perfect competition are monopolistic competition, oligopoly, and monopoly.

This array of markets is generally studied in regard to the
relative efficiency of its components. The problem is said or
assumed to be the satisfaction of the wants of consumers, a
problem we have considered previously and will touch on
again. For the moment, our attention is directed to a special
theoretical requirement of any market, which is that it must

be "cleared," because it is at the theoretical point of clearance that the theoretical supply and demand curves meet. It is easy to see the origin of the requirement in a produce market—especially in a fish market—where what isn't sold in a very short time isn't salable at all. The need to clear the market forces merchants to lower their prices as the day wanes, or to cut prices immediately when it appears that the market is glutted. The need to clear the market thus keeps prices down or, in the case of a shortage, forces them up.

Once we leave the produce markets, however, we seldom again find a market that has to be cleared, and then only in a distress situation. All other markets—including mom-and-pop grocery stores as well as supermarkets—are based on a steady flow of business. They are not cleared; indeed, if they were cleared, they would be out of business. Whatever is sold must be restocked. This is true of every level of trade, from manufacturer, through wholesaler, to retailer.

Perhaps because agriculture in general, like the markets in which its produce is sold, suffers under the constraint of spoilage, contemporary textbooks, with few or no exceptions, illustrate the law of supply and demand with examples from agriculture. Such examples may have been representative enough in the days of Adam Smith and even of Ricardo and Malthus and Mill, but today they are at the fringe—albeit a necessary fringe—of the economy. Thus, in 1980, the American economy totaled $2633.1 billion, while farming and fisheries produced $74.1 billion, or 2.8 percent. To this figure one might reasonably add the tractor and farm-equipment industries, the cost of irrigation and agricultural research, and the substantial share of the petroleum industry that goes into fertilizer and pesticides as well as into tractor fuel. Even including these and, in addition, packing and distributing services, one is forced to the conclusion that agriculture is by no means representative of the modern economy.

Various agricultural agencies publish tables purporting to show the number of bushels of corn that can be sold at various prices, and these tables, when reduced to analytic geom-

etry, produce smooth curves stretching elegantly downward
and to the right. But once the crop is harvested, the supply,
subject to known storage facilities, is fixed and cannot be
increased in answer to a higher price, or decreased in answer to a lower. Next year's supply may conceivably be affected, but not this year's. And, when next year's crop is
harvested, it will be the same thing all over again, except
that then the demand may be different, too.

A farm, moreover, is not an altogether idiosyncratic affair,
because it, too, is an ongoing concern and must be managed
with an eye to its continuing operation in the future. This
year's crop is vital, but next year's crop must also be planned
for. In short, with the possible exception of the produce
markets, commercial exchange is a flow. It is not a series of
discrete haggles, much less of auctions. This does not mean
that individual products or product lines or producers do not
leave the "market" or that others do not enter. It does mean,
however, that entering and leaving are not done as the naïve
law of supply and demand imagines.

As what may seem an extreme example, consider a business deeply involved in shifting taste and fashion, say a
book-publishing house. Every book, as the industry wisdom
has it, is different. With insignificant exceptions, the sale of
Book A is not dependent upon the sale of Book B; they are
read, and sold, independently. In addition, upwards of forty
thousand new books have been published in the United
States in every recent year, so that it is not surprising that
most of these never appear in bookstores, and that the shelf
life of those that do appear is only a few weeks. Although
some books live for centuries, most are almost as ephemeral
as green vegetables in the produce market. Alfred North
Whitehead said that "knowledge keeps no better than fish,"
and the aphorism would seem to apply to books that transmit
knowledge. Yet the book market is not cleared, nor is the
market for a given publisher's books. As fast as one book
goes out of print, another takes its place. Publishers must
publish or perish.

A business concern is a going concern, or it is nothing. Its viability depends on its ability to keep its markets constantly supplied, not cleared. For this obvious reason, the formulation of the law of supply and demand is sometimes modified to read that the market need not be cleared but merely satisfied. The point of satisfaction or equilibrium makes possible a continuing supply for a continuing demand. This formulation, however, reduces the alleged law to a tautology, for the quantity of a good sold must always equal the quantity bought, regardless of the price, and the market is thus "satisfied" at any level.

iv

It is the ruling fashion among contemporary economists to exhibit lack of interest in the conflict between actual price and just price, or between price and value, perhaps because no equation can be devised to resolve it. Yet the relation of price to value is at the center of economic problems. Where price and value are identical, there is no problem; nothing is out of order; nothing needs to be fixed. The vice of inflation is not so much that prices rise as that price-value relationships are distorted. A persistent objective of economic policy is the stabilization of farm prices; if farm values were equally volatile, there would be no injustice in the gyrations.

Society, moreover, has an interest in price that may be different from that of either of the exchangers. In primitive environments a hunter may demand of individuals such returns for his spoils that he puts the band or tribe in thrall. Modern examples are perhaps less dramatic but still ubiquitous: Are the services of any corporation president worth fifty million dollars a year? Are high wages paid steelworkers ruining the industry and damaging the economy? On the other hand, are the wages paid teachers so low that educational standards suffer?

Thus the idea of the just price has persisted. Advocates of any form of price fixing have acted in the name of justice. This was true of the medieval and Renaissance guilds; it is true today of labor unions and proponents of agricultural price supports and metropolitan rent controls. Utility regulation seeks prices that will be fair to both the utilities and the public.

Nor was the idea of justice foreign to that of the free market. The invisible hand was supposed to achieve a result compatible with moral sentiments and so to attain a natural as opposed to a theological justice, a natural price as opposed to a just price. "There is," wrote Adam Smith, "in every society or neighborhood an ordinary or average rate both of wages and profit in every different employment of labour and stock. . . . When the price of any commodity is neither more nor less than what is sufficient to pay the rent of the land, the wages of the labour, and the profits of the stock employed in raising, preparing, and bringing it to market, according to their natural rates, the commodity is then sold for what may be called its natural price."

Smith recognized that, once goods were brought to market, the natural price had nothing to do with the price actually paid. What then controlled was what he called effectual demand, "which is different from the absolute demand. A very poor man may be said in some sense to have a demand for a coach and six; he might like to have it; but his demand is not an effectual demand, as the commodity can never be brought to market in order to satisfy it."

The effectual demand may be so great that "a competition will immediately begin" among those who want and can afford a certain commodity, and this will push the market price above the natural price. And if the effectual demand is weak, competition among sellers will force the market price below the natural price. A high market price will attract new producers to the field; the resulting increased availability of the product will deflate the competition among the buyers; and the price will fall. A low market price will have the opposite effect. So the market will tend toward the natural price, at which point price will be in equilibrium. This is the supposed working of the law of supply and demand that we still talk about.

The so-called law has a necessary condition that is not generally noticed, though Smith mentions it in passing. He puts it this way: "Though the price, therefore, which leaves him his profit, is not always the lowest at which a dealer may sometimes sell his goods, it is the lowest at which he is likely to sell them for any considerable time; at least where there is perfect liberty, or where he may change his trade as often as he pleases." The difficulty with this condition is that while in a free society one may change one's trade as often as one pleases, as a practical matter one can't do so. A mom-and-pop grocery store, run out of business by a supermarket, can't readily shift to sporting goods—or back, if, as not infrequently happens, the supermarket chain is dissatisfied with its new outlet. Nor can the supermarket shift to selling books if the competition becomes too stiff in the grocery business.

Even so, retail trade, which Smith seems to have had in mind, is much more flexible than manufacturing. If you have a steel mill, you can't use it, in a slack season for steel, to refine oil. You can of course buy a company that refines oil, but this merely changes the ownership of the oil company; it does not increase the supply of oil. Hence the move serves no purpose in the supply-and-demand equation. The theory is neat, but in the actual world it is largely irrelevant, because it requires the possibility of instant changes that are instantly effective. Moreover, the theory cannot allow demand to change while supply is changing, or vice versa. What the theory does not allow for is time, time for the market to respond to a given change, and time during which unlooked-for changes occur.

v

All exchanges involve ethical questions. In everyday life we cannot live at a constant fever pitch of deliberation. In a famous chapter in his textbook on psychology William James laid out the importance of habit in allowing us to get on with the business of living without worrying over "which sock, shoe, or trouser-leg [to] put on first." In the same way social customs and trade practices—what Arthur Okun called the invisible handshake—allow us to go about our work without constantly weighing and agonizing over the ethical implications of our actions. Nevertheless, all changes *ipso facto* involve other people and so by their very nature present ethical questions. A virtuous act enlarges the person and a vicious act contradicts some enlargement. "I could not love thee, dear, so much, loved I not honour more" expresses conflict but not contradiction. A rational exchange looks to the maintenance of both trading partners, but nineteenth-century Social Darwinism and the twentieth-century theory of games (among many examples) contemplate the destruction of one partner by the other and hence the destruction of exchange and the repudiation of its genesis. This is irrational and vicious.

Exchanging goods and services is only one of the principal ways of meeting other minds, of being recognized by others, of recognizing oneself, of becoming conscious of one's limits and so of one's powers. We meet one another as buyers and sellers, as teachers and pupils, as patrons and clients, as friends, as lovers, and also as competitors and enemies. Society depends on these relationships. Individuality as we know it depends on them. Their development has been a work of history. They have not always been as they are now. Even a hundred years ago loving was much different from what it is today, as can be seen by comparing Anthony Trollope's *Phineas Redux* with John Updike's *Rabbit Redux*. The differences in ways of economic exchanging are, if anything, greater.

Without noneconomic interests, economic interests are sterile and shapeless. Without economic interests, noneconomic interests are abstract. Different sorts of exchange—and also different possible exchanges of the same sort—are in conflict with each other. The meaning of a commitment is understood only as it conflicts with another. The conflict results not in the obliteration of one by the other, nor in a trade-off that diminishes both, but in a comprehension that modifies and may intensify both. An unconflicted commitment is obsession or madness. A resolved conflict is personality: one resolves to be the person one becomes. The controls of economic activity are those that maintain not only the economic modes but the other modes as well—that maintain and rationalize the conflicts among them. This is neither altruism nor prudence but brings us back to self-maintenance and self-assertion.

7

LABOR

Where It All Begins

i

From the beginning, it was obvious that the invisible hand was less than perfect, and that the models it propelled didn't quite run right. Anyone could see that some unworthy things were overpriced and some worthy things under-priced. Prices, moreover, were not constant but fluctuated even from hour to hour. No science could be expected to develop in the midst of such turmoil.

If price didn't afford a stable definition of value, where could stability be found? The great economists have all been essentially decent men. The meaning of the myth of Midas has not been lost on them, nor have they been able to stomach the proposition that a miser fingering his hoard is the pinnacle toward which civilization has been building. On the other side, they are all children of the Reformation; they are all celebrants of the work ethic; and they all, in themselves, exhibit the acclaim accorded to achievers.

With this background it is not surprising that they have all been persuaded that the true, the real, the fundamental, the everlasting standard of value is labor. The theme is announced by Adam Smith: "Labour alone, therefore, never varying in its own value, is alone the ultimate and real standard by which the value of all commodities can at all times and places be estimated and compared. It is their real price;

75

money is their nominal price only." (The words "real" and "nominal" aren't the same as those of medieval philosophy, but they do give rise to similar difficulties.)

Smith's successors stated the labor theory of value in terms somewhat different from his. Where Smith had said that labor was the standard of value of the commodities the laborer received, Ricardo argued that the issue was the commodities labor produced. Keynes held that "the unit of labor" was "the sole physical unit which we require in our economic system." Marx was in general agreement: "How, then, is the magnitude of [use-value] to be measured? Plainly by the quantity of the value-creating substance, the labour, contained in the article."

Labor is a curious standard of value in that, unlike money, it can scarcely be a store of value. Nor is it easy to say exactly what labor is. The army sometimes taught rambunctious soldiers to mind their manners by having them dig a hole six feet wide, six feet long, and six feet deep, and then fill it up again. There was plenty of labor involved in the exercise, but not much economic consequence. Perhaps, then, it wasn't really labor, but only labor in a manner of speaking, that is to say, nominally. Similar problems arise in trying to find a common measure of skilled labor and unskilled labor, efficient labor and inefficient labor, mental labor and menial labor, labor paid and unpaid, earnest labor and time-serving.

Consider the CEO of a *Fortune* 500 company, who has six or eight division presidents "reporting" to him, but really running the company, as much as anybody does. From sheer boredom he may throw himself into politicking somewhere, or he may throw the company into a frenzy of mergers and take-overs and spin-offs. Either way, the net consequence is not much greater than the soldier's six-by-six-by-six hole in the ground. In what sense is the soldier or the CEO laboring? How can their disparate laboring be a universal standard of value?

There are two ways of reducing what they do to a common denominator. The first is to accept their pay as the yardstick, or perhaps some ingenious accounting of the value they add to production; but such a solution equates money values with real values, and it was precisely to avoid this equation that the notion of a labor standard was introduced. The other possible measuring unit is time: the unit of labor is an hour of laboring. This is the solution Marx adopts in his theory of surplus value, where he argues that the distinction between skilled and unskilled labor is confused, that skilled labor is relatively insignificant, and that the capitalist appropriates the same proportion of the output of skilled and unskilled labor, anyhow. "We therefore," he concludes, "save our- selves a superfluous operation, and simplify our analysis, by the assumption that the labour of the workman employed by the capitalist is unskilled average labour."

Even this simplification has to be underwritten by concern to define "average labour." On a spread of two pages of *Capital* we find peppered the following adjectives: "useful," "normal," "suitable," "socially necessary," "normal" again, "average," "normal" yet again, "average" again, and "usual." This of course is an array of synonyms rather than a defini- tion. Marx does, indeed, give a definition, and it is a sur- prise: The capitalist, he says, "has bought the use of the labour-power for a definite period, and he insists on his rights. He has no intention of being robbed." And so on. Thus "average labour" is what the capitalist, backed by his penal code, says it is; it is not a "scientific" standard at all. Even with Marx, the values of capitalism are *asserted* by the capitalist.

ii

If labor is not a standard, is it then a commodity? Marx, as a matter of fact, thought it was, at least in the capitalist mode of production. Capital, he wrote, "can spring into life, only when the owner of the means of production and subsistence meets in the market with the free labourer selling his labour- power." For labor power to be a salable commodity, Marx held that it had to be "free" (by which he meant unrestricted), and that the laborer had to be "free" (that is, unconnected and without resources).

If we accept these conditions, we may doubt whether Marx's scenario was ever staged in its pure form. Since his time, in any event, the capitalist nations have all enacted not only minimum-wage laws but also laws governing child labor and hours and conditions of work and vacations and unemployment compensation and old-age security and freedom to join labor unions and much else. And all such laws implicitly recognize that labor is different from, and should be treated differently from, ordinary commodities.

In another sense labor is not an ordinary commodity. It cannot be alienated more than once. An ordinary commodity can be sold and resold until it wears out, but free laborers' time can be sold only once. They work from sun to sun, and tomorrow is another day. The employer who "buys" today's time cannot sell it to someone else, who might in turn resell it. There are of course exceptions: slavery and peonage (which are different modes and so don't count), certain sports and entertainment contracts, and some hiring practices, especially of farmhands and longshoremen. All of these are limited in their incidence.

If labor is not a commodity, and if it is not a standard either, what is it? It is what no one will ordinarily question, essential. It is fundamental, primary, irreducible, original, basic, ontological. It is, moreover, human. We do with it what we will; we will what we do with it. How we labor is one of the principal ways in which we assert ourselves. We define ourselves by what we do and how we do it and how we treat the doings of others.

iii

Labor may not be a commodity; yet we expect to be paid for our work. The program of "From each according to his abilities, to each according to his needs," first enunciated by

Louis Blanc, then publicized by Marx in his *Critique of the Gotha Program*, and finally enshrined in the Soviet constitution, has not had broad appeal, at least among those with the abilities to make themselves heard. Even the towering prestige of Mao Zedong could not advance the idea much beyond sloganeering. We must assert ourselves in the world and must likewise look there for recognition.

The laborer who makes the most insistent—and usually richly rewarded—claim to recognition is the entrepreneur. Historically, the entrepreneur was both capitalist and executive. Adam Smith and Karl Marx and John Stuart Mill, if they made the distinction at all, thought of the latter as a sort of overseer or foreman or clerk of the works or supercargo. He represented the owners, was an extension of their will, followed their orders. Occasionally he was able to accumulate funds of his own, whereupon he became a capitalist in his own right and abandoned his subservient position.

This structure, which was comfortably suited to individual proprietorships, partnerships, and even joint stock companies, was carried over, in the latter half of the nineteenth century, to the new limited-liability company. Arguing from one analogy or another, legislatures and courts developed a theory of the corporation whereby each share of stock, like each citizen of a democracy, had a vote in the election of the directors, who acted as a sort of legislature, established company policy, and hired the managers to execute that policy.

Even as this theory was being developed, it was recognized as a legal fiction. Subsequent critics, like R. H. Tawney, emphasized the corporate divorce between ownership and work. A. A. Berle and Gardiner C. Means documented the passing of control of the typical corporation from stockholders and directors to management. The shift of control to management tended, as John Kenneth Galbraith argued, to change corporate objectives from profit maximization to the protection of what he called the planning system and its technicians.

Joseph A. Schumpeter was probably mistaken in seeing these changes as the result of "technological progress." Business may indeed, as he said, be increasingly conducted by "teams of trained specialists who turn out what is required and make it work in predictable ways." There is also much evidence that "Bureau and committee work tends to replace individual action." But it is not true that "the leading man . . . is becoming just another office worker—and one who is not always difficult to replace."

The leading man has not in fact sunk into gray anonymity, as he would have done if his role had actually been reduced by technological progress. He is as colorful and as active as ever. His activities have been redirected, as Keynes understood, not by technology, but by the development of the stock exchanges. In Chapter 12 of *The General Theory*, Keynes observed that "there is no sense in building up a new enterprise at a cost greater than that at which a similar enterprise can be purchased; whilst there is inducement to spend on a new project what may seem an extravagant sum, if it can be floated off on the Stock Exchange at an immediate profit. Thus certain classes of investment [a footnote explained that these classes include practically all investment] are governed by the average expectation of those who deal on the Stock Exchange as revealed in the price of shares rather than by the genuine expectations of the professional entrepreneur."

The triumph of speculation over enterprise does not, of course, eliminate the human element. The leading man (in Schumpeter's phrase), no matter what kind of activity he leads, still needs animal spirits (in Keynes's). Someone must undertake to do whatever is done. It is convenient to continue to call him (or, it may be, her) the entrepreneur, even though some of his or her activities would not be recognized by Marx or Mill.

The entrepreneurial function, Schumpeter wrote, "does not necessarily consist in either inventing anything or otherwise creating the conditions which the enterprise exploits. It consists in getting things done." The person with the special and comparatively rare talent that satisfies this function was earlier characterized by Frank H. Knight as an economic surd. No perfectly prudent person is an entrepreneur; the risks of failure are too obvious and too great. As Keynes said, "If human nature felt no temptation to take a chance, no satisfaction (profit apart) in constructing a railway, a mine or a farm, there might not be much investment merely as a result of cold calculation."

All of this is true; yet it is not impossible that the case for the entrepreneur has been overstated. There may be no industry without him, but industry depends also on those who toil in the vineyard; and it has occurred to many to wonder whether all that toil is necessary or desirable. Hesiod's *Works and Days*, which might be said to be the first economics text, as well as one of the oldest of literary works to come down to us, announces a theme that still teases mankind. After an invocation to Zeus, Hesiod laments:

> From men the source of life has been hidden well.
> Else you would lightly do enough work in a day
> To keep you the rest of the year while you lounged at play.

More recently the same idea inspired Thoreau to retreat to Walden Pond, and more recently still, so-called alternate lifestyles have been celebrated.

Against these seductive notions, it has been argued that Thoreau's experiment depended not only on Emerson's support but also on the industries that originally produced the shanty boards and secondhand windows and one thousand old bricks that he bought secondhand. Somebody worked at those industries, even though Thoreau didn't. Even Marx advanced a similar argument, contending that the historical role of capitalism was the rationalization of production necessary to make decent work and leisure generally available in the communist future. It is unquestionable that grinding poverty was the common lot in the Western world until very recently.

It is, however, equally unquestionable that hunters and gatherers, where they still exist, live comparatively toil-free lives, and that an appropriate ordering of priorities would enable even a New Yorker to work a stress-free thirty-five hours a week and have twice that time free for libraries and museums and botanical gardens and such. It would therefore seem necessary to recognize that the common laborer is as much an economic surd as the entrepreneur. They are both essential for the work of the world; but there is no reason why either should work so hard at it—no reason, that is, except that work is one of the ways in which we define ourselves.

iv

In the meantime, entrepreneurs and managers are paid very well, and common laborers are paid very poorly. One man was paid $51 million in 1982, another took down more than $44 million, and a third made do with $15 million. There were several dozen others (not counting rock singers and sports stars) who got more than a million. These sums were compensation for one year's labor and are said to have been earned. (It may be assumed that they were also snugly sheltered, but that is another question.) Even *Fortune* magazine suggested in 1983 that things were getting out of hand (though it changed its mind a year later).

When justification is sought for such astronomical sums, attention is usually called to the responsibilities accepted by the corporation CEO. If a workman on the assembly line makes a mistake, it is likely to be caught by someone else; and even if it isn't, the possible damage is limited. But if the CEO makes a wrong decision, he may bankrupt the company. Furthermore, the workman cannot make a *correct* decision that is more than routine, while the CEO may, with a clever move, multiply the company's earnings many times.

The importance and difficulty of all this decision making is certainly overrated. As Galbraith points out, difficult decisions usually are difficult because they are close, and close decisions tend to be close because there is not much to choose between the alternative possibilities. In such situations, it doesn't make much difference which way the ball bounces. Really important decisions, on the other hand, decisions that do make a difference, are often blindingly obvious.

That this analysis is in general correct is indicated by customary corporate practice. Apologists for big business—especially those inimical to government—are fond of contrasting the risky career of the business executive with the life tenure of the civil servant (in such discussions the volatile life of the elected official is not mentioned). As a matter of fact, however, it is rare for a CEO to be dismissed for malfeasance, let alone misfeasance or nonfeasance. In most companies it would be lèse majesté to suggest that the old man had made a mistake. The life of a CEO is so stable that it caused some fluttering when Robert Townsend suggested in *Up the Organization* that the term of a corporation president ought to be no more than five years. If decision making were all that difficult, a CEO's life would not be such a happy one.

Though the difficulty of decision making may be exaggerated, it is true that most people are willing to let someone else do it. Successful business executives do display a willingness to make decisions, however easy or difficult, and are rewarded for that. In addition, they are said to have valuable experience to call on. Again there is something to the argument, but again perhaps less than is claimed for it. For it is reasonable to inquire how they came by all that experience. They were, as the saying goes, lucky enough to be in the right place at the right time, and not uncommonly they inherited the right place.

In any case, as people climb the corporate ladder, several important things are being tested beyond their ability to do sums in their heads and their cheerful willingness to anticipate what their boss wants. Perhaps most important of all, they are exhibiting their ability to learn, and especially their ability to understand at a glance how things work. If they're going to get ahead, they've got to have a quick ear and a sharp eye.

It must be acknowledged that the quick ear and the sharp

eye are far from common. At the same time, it is possible that we may have here another of those nature vs. nurture problems, like the debate over whether women are naturally slow at mathematics or merely are brought up that way. One's genetic composition (whatever that may mean), home environment, and formal education may be of the most promising, but a few years in the lower reaches of a large organization that happens to be riddled with office politics can be devastating. The winners in such contests prove themselves adept at politics; and if they're good at their jobs too, that's a plus. The losers' talents never have a chance to develop.

The winners, in fair contests as well as in foul, gain something more than pay raises. They gain experience. They have increased opportunities to practice the use of their eyes and ears. They learn by doing. Perhaps more important, they join C. Wright Mills's "power elite" and gradually expand their business connections so that they are eventually on familiar terms with the most "useful" people among their firm's customers, suppliers, and competitors. All of this makes them—or seems to make them—many times more valuable to their firms than the inexperienced, dispirited, though almost equally talented, losers. And this is said to justify the enormous difference in their salaries.

There is also, in the minds of the directors who formally set the high CEO salaries, another justification. They believe that they must pay their CEO well, or he (it's almost always "he") will decamp for some competitor that does pay well (after all, he knows them all), thus subtracting his skills from their company and adding them to the competition. It is not impossible that this reasoning is sound, especially since paying him an extra million, say, to hold him, is just a drop in a *Fortune* 500 bucket. Moreover, if he really and truly can increase his firm's profit by a million and one dollars (and who's to say he can't?), he will have proved, as classical economists say, the marginal utility of his raise.

This reasoning may remind us of the free-agent auction in baseball. And indeed the same principles operate, with the same results: astronomical salaries for a few stars, who are expected to attract the crowds, whopping raises to keep the most important and most powerful of the rest in line, and higher prices for the paying customers. This is a curious situation in which one individual, or a very small group, can have what Professor Galbraith calls countervailing power against a very large corporation, or even against the economy as a whole.

v

At this point it may repay us to look a little more closely at the compensation of one of these fortunate few. Let us suppose a bright and well-educated young man of twenty-one, who does not inherit his position but is thought to be of "management potential." In the present state of the business world, it would not be quite realistic to suppose a young woman in the same situation. So a young man. He starts work for a *Fortune* 500 company, not as an apprentice sweeping the factory floor, nor even as a clerk running errands in accounts receivable, but as a management trainee. He is by no means at the bottom of the ladder, but it's still a long way to the top, and at every rung he's in head-to-head competition with others like himself, many from outside his company (and he may shift companies himself). If he gets to be CEO at age fifty-one, he will have prevailed in perhaps ten such contests—a competition rather like a tennis-club ladder, in which one periodically challenges the player above or is challenged by the player below.

At any rate, our man finally makes it to the top. The question now is, How much better was he than his competitors? The difference may be thinner than a double-edge razor blade. Jimmy Connors was undisputed 1982 Wimbledon champion, but he and John McEnroe won the same number of games in the final match and even scored the same number of points. Beyond that it is, as the announcers say, a game of inches.

Let's give our man all the credit we can. Let's suppose that, at each rung of the ladder, he shows himself 10 percent better than his competition. That is, one must admit, a pretty big margin if he runs into any competition at all. So if we give our hero an even 10 percent superiority at every stage, we're not understating his attainments.

On this assumption it is reasonable to claim that when he finally pulls himself to the top, he has proved himself ten times 1.1 times (1.1^{10}), or 2.59 times, better than the losers in the first contest. Thus it would seem reasonable for his pay to be 2.59 times better than theirs. If the permanent losers, with modest seniority raises, got themselves up to $30,000 at age fifty-one, the winning CEO should be earning 2.59 times that, or $77,700. Giving him the breakage, it would be $77,812.

This is of course ridiculous. There is no *Fortune* 500 CEO who doesn't make many times $77,812, without even thinking of fringe benefits, options, and other perquisites. The man who was paid $51 million in 1982 got 665 times the amount we've calculated for a more run-of-the-mill CEO. (If you want to state that really dramatically, you can say that the former was 65,500 percent of the latter.) And consider: $51 million is 1,700 times (170,000 percent) the pay of the losers in the race, who were no fools to begin with, or about 5,400 times (540,000 percent) the poverty level for a family of four.

It is doubtful that anyone really believes that these fantastic differentials can be justified on any basis of amount of work or difficulty of work or contribution to the general welfare. It is sometimes contended, not without a show of reasonableness, that if a foreman (or -woman) supervising six or eight workers receives a paycheck one or two thousand dollars higher than theirs, the CEO supervising sixty or eighty thousand workers is entitled to a proportionately higher reward. Or if the CEO of a firm with annual profits of a million dollars takes home fifty thousand a year (and probably much more), the CEO of a company earning a billion dollars would be entitled to take home fifty million. Of course, he never does (our $51-million-a-year man was with a much smaller company). One reason why he doesn't is that the CEO is actually supervising not sixty or eighty thousand people, but six or eight subsidiary presidents, who in turn supervise six or eight vice presidents, who in turn supervise six or eight division heads, and so on down the line. This is, moreover, the chain of command; the CEO has an extensive staff to assist him, and so do all of his subordinates, except those at the end of the line.

In the end, the argument is that in a free country with a free market, one is entitled to get whatever the market will bear. If the demand is great, it is right to reap the benefit of that demand. If there is strong demand for computer programmers, and if few are available, competition will push their salaries up. The same is true of common laborers, though they tend to get pushed in the other direction. It is all a question of supply and demand.

So it is said. One would have to be a fool not to be aware that given the way a modern corporation is set up, the CEO and those at the top can pretty much write their own tickets or, to change the figure, design their own golden parachutes. It is difficult to contemplate some recent performances of this sort without outrage and disgust. But this is not our present point. For the moment it is enough to observe that when you rely on the market to justify your salary, you are reducing your labor—and yourself—to a commodity, a mere thing.

vi

The aims of a human life are, as Freud said, loving and working. These are two of the ways in which we declare our membership in society and acknowledge our obligations. These declarations and acknowledgments are not passive; they must be actively pursued, and in this some are more fortunate than others.

On the other side, one has no obligation that is not confirmed by rights. Society can do little about loving—except to refrain from admitting impediments—but working is at the very heart of it. A political economy that fails to allow its citizens to contribute to the common weal fails fundamentally.

This is not a matter of prudence or of benefit-cost analysis. The citizen's right to make a contribution is absolute, as absolute as society's right to hold him or her to obedience to the laws. No one has a right to a particular job with a particular firm, but everyone has a right to make a contribution. As a consequence, the state must be, as used to be said, the employer of last resort. The last resort is not the citizen's but the state's. It is the state's obligation to enable its citizens to advance the state's purposes. In this, as in so much else, the New Deal was creative and prophetic, and the postwar years have seen a steady erosion of morale.

The problem is not, as the nineteenth century conceived it, one of forcing people to work by threatening starvation. Nor is it one of enticing people to work by promising rewards. As Galbraith showed in *The Affluent Society*, the economy can proceed very efficiently with large numbers of potential workers on the dole. But the citizens cannot proceed in that way.

vii

Self-justification—not market justification—is crucial if self-assertion is the ground of labor. It would be absurd to find one's meaning in one's work and at the same time to declare the work unworthy. Such absurdity does, however, abound, whence the banal apology of the businessman caught in sharp or mean practice, that he's not in it for his health.

Searching for the legitimization of private property, John Locke wrote, "As much land as a man tills, plants, improves, cultivates, and can use the product of, so much is his property." He felt that a man's legitimate possessions were limited to what he could produce and use before it spoiled, but he granted that money as a store of value allowed one to pile up as much as one had a mind to. This piling up, it may be noted, was to be strictly in money, not in producers' goods. As early as Aristotle, however, it had been seen that the "so-called art of money-making" had no limit. This of course was a fatal defect to the Greek mind. Those who practiced this art were, Aristotle said, "intent on living only, and not upon living well; and as their desires are unlimited, they also de-sire that the means of gratifying them should be without limit." Such people are with us still. The other day the son of a Texas oil multimillionaire dropped out of college, went to work for his father, and in short order had made some mil-lions on his own. The father was asked why the son needed to do this. "What else is there to do?" was the rejoinder.

In all candor, it must be admitted that this sort of thinking is perfectly congruent with the introductory paragraphs of many (if not most) of today's economics-principles texts. In terms of desires or wants or material gain, there is no limit to money making or the bottom line or, for that matter, the GNP. No invisible hand guides them. The compensation of labor—executive labor as well as common labor—has no "natural" standard; it is not a "scientific" question. It is an expression of the standards, the ideals, the will of society and its members. It is an ethical question. It goes to our mores, our morale, our morals.

Labor is not a commodity, or a standard, or a means to an ulterior end, but an end in itself. Economic labor is what you do for money. There are many things you do where money is no consideration. There are, in fact, many people who never do anything for money. From this fact it follows that economics cannot be all of life. It is an essential factor in our civilization—in our historical situation—but there are other factors.

What you are paid money for is the production of goods, which may include the rendering of services. Our next ques-tion will concern these goods and their consumption.

8

GOODS

Where It All Ends

i

What makes a "good" good? An answer that leaps to mind is that an economic good can be judged according to its usefulness. The literature is indeed full of discussion of use values, which are distinguished in various ways from exchange values and from labor values or cost values. Having been brought up when pragmatism was in flower, we may be inclined to believe that use value is the only thing. Money, as everyone from Adam Smith on has said, is only good for what you can buy with it (and what you can buy with money is only good for what you can do with it). As consumption is the physical end of production, it is held to be the rational end, too (though not by Marx, who was perhaps the original supply sider). This would seem to be only common sense; but usefulness is as elusive a concept when applied to goods as we have found it when applied to labor. The soldier's digging of that six-by-six-by-six hole in the ground wasn't useful labor because the hole wasn't useful, but useful holes are certainly dug.

Classical economists carried the analysis a step further. The consumer, as they observed, is also the producer; and if he doesn't consume, he is unable to produce. Hence the wage level cannot long fall below the level at which labor can subsist and also reproduce itself. Competition, Ricardo emphasized, will see to it that the minimum wage is also the maximum. On the other side, if wages rise even a little above subsistence, the laboring classes will improvidently have more children, thus increasing the competition for jobs and bringing wages down again.

This analysis is of course nonsense. As Malthus pointed out, having his friend Ricardo in mind, "an increase of labourers cannot be brought into the market, in consequence of a particular demand, till after the lapse of sixteen or eighteen years." A lot can happen in that length of time. We have in fact seen the theory refuted in the history of our postwar baby boom, which in the first place surely had as much to do with pent-up longing as with pent-up purchasing power, and which in the second place resulted in an enormous surge in employment, production, and real wages. The surge was reversed, not by demographic forces, but by the Federal Reserve Board.

When we talk of economic goods, we have more than subsistence in mind, anyhow. Subsistence, as we have remarked, is a physiological problem. Even for Ricardo, the subsisting laborers were producing something more than their own and their employers' subsistence. What made that something good? That question includes "how" and "why" questions, which we will take up in order.

ii

In answering the first question, let us begin by inquiring how a service becomes an economic good. That nothing intrinsic to the service makes it an economic good a few examples will show. Home cooking of the highest quality is not an economic good, but hash slinging of junk food is an economic good. Home handy work is not an economic good, but hired plumbing is. The money you save by staining furniture you buy unfinished is not an economic good, but the extra you pay for finished furniture represents an economic good. Whether you pray standing in the corners of the street or in your closet with the door closed, what you do is not an economic good; but when a priest or parson prays for you, that is. It is even possible to argue that our hapless soldier digging that hole in the ground is performing an economic service, since he does it in the line of duty, for which he is paid.

An economic service, accordingly, is work done for pay, regardless of what else may be said about it. The service may be good, bad, or indifferent—performed shoddily or with grace. It may be one of general usefulness, as maintaining telephone communications. It may be one of idiosyncratic usefulness, as praying for the faithful. It may be one of nil or negative usefulness, as offering me cream and sugar for my coffee in a restaurant. All that matters is that it be done for pay. Since it certainly is not uncommon for people to be so delighted with their work that they do it for pleasure, it may be more precise to say that an economic service is paid service.

This insistence on pay is not arbitrary. The alternative is to consider everything anyone does—at least everything that involves two or more people—as economic. Such analyses quickly reduce to such absurdities as Marx's theory that slavery is latent in the family or the variation of this theory that sees marriage as an exchange of sexual favors for security. That some marriages may seem like that, even to the partners, says nothing about most marriages, and certainly nothing about any humanistic view of marriage. Furthermore, if such an exchange were truly economic, one would have to look for the resulting income, which could be stated only in money. Without an actual monetary exchange, the statement would be arbitrary, and the taxing authorities would be dragged into foolish calculations. If the husband leapt from the marriage bed to prepare breakfast, would his wife's income be greater than if he turned over and went back to sleep? If so, by how much?

Insistence on a monetary transaction makes an economic service an ephemeral good. It doesn't exist unless it is done and paid for; and once it is done, that is the end of it. They also serve who only stand and wait—provided they are paid for it. An unemployed waiter produces no economic value. Nor can services be stockpiled. In slack times, or in anticipation of a strike, I cannot make extra rides up and down in the office elevator and so be prepared for crowded or nonexistent service to come. We have already noted that labor power—the power to perform a service—cannot be resold.

In all this, services seem different from material goods. But the difference can be made too much of, for all material goods are also more or less ephemeral. Not only do moth and rust corrupt and thieves break in and steal, but material things may lose their marketability, which, in fact, many material things never have.

Prompted by personal enthusiasm, by the acclaim of respected critics—by any number of things—a book publisher may produce more copies of a novel than he can sell at any price. There may be several thousand left after the regular sale at the full price and even after the remainder sale at the lowest price that repays the cost of handling. In the end, to make room in the warehouse, the rest are shredded if there is a sufficient need for waste paper, dumped in a "sanitary" landfill otherwise.

This is not an esoteric scenario in the book business, and it has myriad parallels in other lines, even under communism. In the heyday of the Gang of Four, several streets of Shanghai were lined with hundreds or thousands of good-sized steel boilers quietly rusting under the plane trees. Somebody had no doubt been praised for exceeding his quota, but what he produced (if not still there) has had to be reduced to scrap. These things happen, whether as a result of American know-how or in accordance with Mao Zedong Thought, because no one can foretell the future.

Were the books, as they were bulldozed into the landfill, or the boilers, as they were crushed and melted down, goods? They were material, all right. You could touch them, see them, smell them, weigh them, measure them, determine their chemical composition. But they were not goods.

They were goods for a while, but their goodness was evanescent.

This evanescence of goodness calls attention to the way in which a good is created. The novel was an economic good (we are not commenting on its literary merit), not because of the labor (that did the writing and tended the machines that made the paper and printed the books), the land (whose trees were made into paper), the capital (that provided the paper mill, and the printing press, and the warehouse for the publisher's inventory), or whatever other factors of production you care to name. All these were necessary, but they were not sufficient to create a good. The factors of production resulted in an artifact, not an economic good.

The artifact became an economic good as it passed from hand to hand through the economic system. The passing did not have to be constant, but it did have to have a constant potentiality. Once the possibility of movement was foreclosed or abandoned or ended, the economic value of the artifact vanished.

At every stage, the product depends on the system, and the system is prior. While today's product may modify tomorrow's system, it could have been produced only because today's system was a going concern. The system includes the market but is not confined to that; there is scarcely an aspect of the society and its government that does not bear on it. Putting it in its most obvious terms: an automobile is worthless without roads and gasoline and people who know how to drive. The Inca's hoard, as we have remarked, was worth nothing to him in the face of the destruction of his society; with distribution facilities destroyed, a stock of corn would have done him no better. Goods and services have no economic value unless they are available to an effective demand. The author of our landfilled novel has friends and relatives unable to find the book in a convenient bookstore. The sales are lost; rather, they never existed, and so many more books go to the shredder or dump. Many things for which there is a brisk demand in one society are unsalable at any price in another. Few refrigerators are sold to Eskimos living on ice floes, or so we are given to understand.

The wealth of a nation consists not in its mass of material things but in its system. The natural resources of South America are not inferior to those of the United States, but the wealth of the two regions is vastly different. The land of India is far richer than that of Japan, but the comparative wealth of the two nations is reversed.

Nor is accumulated capital crucial. As John Stuart Mill pointed out, capital is constantly being consumed and re-produced, and this fact explains "what has so often excited wonder, the great rapidity with which countries recover from a state of devastation; the disappearance, in a short time, of all traces of the mischiefs done by earthquakes, floods, hurricanes, and the ravages of war." In 1871 the fledgling German Empire imposed a five-billion-franc war indemnity on France, intending to impoverish her for a gen-eration; but in spite of the loss of Alsace and Lorraine, and in spite of the disorders following the Paris Commune, the en-tire debt was paid off in two years. At the end of World War II, Germany was in ruins, but in short order it became again one of the most prosperous nations of the world—and this without the eastern provinces.

What is true of national wealth is true of goods. What counts is system, a going concern.

iii

"Consumption is the sole end and purpose of all production," wrote Adam Smith, "and the interest of the producer ought to be attended to only so far as may be necessary for promot-ing that of the consumer. The maxim," he added, "is so per-fectly self-evident that it would be absurd to attempt to prove it." The maxim certainly does seem self-evident; why bother to produce something that's not going to be used? Yet in the history of economics the maxim has been remarkably little attended to. Smith himself noted that "in the mercan-tile system, the interest of the consumer is almost constantly sacrificed to that of the producer." The same was true of medieval guilds; it was true of Karl Marx, who insisted that distribution was not the issue; it was true of Andrew Carnegie, who amassed wealth in order to give it away, and of Thorstein Veblen, who satirized the conspicuous consumption of Carnegie's contemporaries; it is true today of Marx's followers, who inveigh against consumerism, and also of the supply-siders, who think of themselves as exemplary anti-Marxists.

This anomalous situation no doubt has roots, as R. H. Tawney suggested, in the Church's doctrines of the sins of avarice and gluttony. The rival teachings of Calvinism had, surprisingly, a similar effect. Salvation was solely a question of divine election; mundane triumph was a possible forecast of election; therefore it was only prudent to work very hard to give the forecast a chance to show itself. At the same time, it was imprudent to enjoy the fruits of the triumphant labor, because anyone who did so obviously valued this world more than the next and so could scarcely be one of the elect. Thus predestination led to vigorous emphasis on production and to studied indifference to consumption. As in the case with success in every line of endeavor, the example of Calvinist businessmen had a widening influence on others of other faiths or of no faith. We have already met the Texas oil multimillionaire whose son left college to make his own millions. "What else is there to do?"

In spite of the self-evident priority of consumption, Adam Smith placed his emphasis, like the others, on production. The title of his book was *An Inquiry into the Nature and Causes of the Wealth of Nations*; he did not promise a discussion of the uses of wealth, nor did he supply any. Given the state of the world then—given the state of the world now—the overwhelming problem has been to produce enough to feed, clothe, and shelter the huddled masses of the earth. Until that problem is solved, it seems frivolous to fuss about the purposes of wealth. But the fact remains that most economic activity is neither directly nor indirectly concerned with the subsistence problem. Economic theory likewise has its mind on higher things; and when it thinks of consumption at all, as Ricardo and Malthus did, it concludes that the mass of mankind is forever condemned to abject poverty, like it or not, while the work of producing the pleasures of the rich and well-born provides employment for the poor. There is no suggestion that these pleasures, whether dainty or coarse, serve otherwise than as a goad to envy, ambition, and emulation. Very few contemporary economists have felt that consumption has to be accounted for at all, except as an offset to saving.

iv

Since economists devote little or no attention to the question of why a thing or service can be considered a good they have no ground for saying that one good is better than another. If one good is not better than another, there is no ground for saying that one allocation of resources is better than another. If one allocation of resources is not better than another, there is no ground for saying that one economic policy is better than another. The attempt to avoid passing judgment is perhaps a corollary of the notion that economics is a science. In any case, it deprives economic analyses of focus and economists' recommendations of urgency and even of relevance.

Unless some wants are judged more worthy of satisfaction than others, no reason can be given for organizing society in such a way as to satisfy my wants or your wants or the wants of a majority of citizens. If wants are absolute, there is no choosing among them, and there is no justice in requiring me to forgo some of mine that may be idiosyncratic in order to satisfy some shared by a majority, no matter how large, that does not include me. I can be forced or persuaded to accept such a situation, but there is no justice in it.

If wants are absolute, an economic system whose purpose is to do the best it can toward satisfying them can be organized in one of two ways. Either a fantastic voting procedure can be devised whereby the electorate picks out what it wants and the government tries its hardest to give satisfaction, or it can be argued—as it is in fact argued—that a free market like the one we have is the most efficient way of doing the job.

It is important to understand what both solutions entail. Give or take a little quibbling, what either the voting or the market comes up with must be considered good. To be sure, there might be more of it; but whatever it is, it is, by definition, good. No other definition is suggested by the theory. Consequently most economists, like Candide after his encounter with Dr. Pangloss's teachings, busy themselves with maximizing production.

But as in the case of constructing indices, it is not so easy to avoid making judgments. The most enthusiastic advocate of production *à outrance* will hesitate over agricultural practices that maximize this year's crop but deplete the topsoil. He understands that overcutting the forests of the Himalayas will result in floods in India and crop failures in Bangladesh. The amount of production, in short, cannot be stated except within a time frame, and there is nothing sacrosanct about the calendar. Indeed, it is now fashionable to argue that American industry has faltered because executives have been maximizing short-term gains. On the other hand, who is eager for pie in the sky by and by?

Even if the time question were satisfactorily solved, there would still remain the problem of counting. How do we know that production is being increased? The problem looks simple enough for a book publisher or a boilermaker: just compare the number of books or boilers produced this year with the number produced last year. But we have seen some of the books shredded and some of the boilers scrapped. Very well, one can count what's left. Counting will work well enough provided what is counted is homogeneous, as would be the case with a small foundry making only one style and size of boiler. But even a very small publisher will publish many different sizes and kinds of books, and it appears that they are not thought of in terms of size or weight or number of pages or number of words or number of anything. A think-piece on economics will cost more, word for word, than a popular novel, regardless of intrinsic merit.

We have drifted from adding up numbers of things to adding up prices of things; there is no other way to solve our problem. But is this a rational solution? If prices are what matter, it is no trick at all to increase them. Anyone could do it in a trice, simply by increasing the money supply or, as they say, by debasing the currency. This has been done more than once in the history of the world. It has even been done in reverse: when in the 1950s France exchanged one new franc for ten old francs, did that cut French production by 90 percent?

Now, this is all obvious enough, and economists have long since solved the problem to their satisfaction by the construction of indices. But we have noted that such constructions all depend on judgment. There is no shirking the responsibility of judging. Even when the responsibility is refused at the start of analysis, it presents itself again and again. The persistence of the problem is a reliable indication that the initial refusal to accept responsibility was illicit, and that wants are not absolute but are liable to judgment.

I cannot be judged—nor can I judge myself—except on what I *do*. Consumption, in short, to the extent that it is not merely physiological, is an activity. It is as much an activity as is production. The consumer is, like the entrepreneur or laborer, an economic surd, a human being. No one is driven by necessity to work as hard as producers do. No one is driven by necessity to consume as much as consumers do. Production and consumption are acts of will, not of necessity.

What, then, is it that consumers do? How can these doings be judged?

v

Thorstein Veblen judged the behavior of consumers, especially those with a great deal to consume, very severely. His position was that the economic "struggle is substantially a race for reputability on the basis of an invidious comparison." What he called "the habit of pecuniary emulation" was not the only motive for economic activity, but all other motives were "greatly affected" by it. In order to demonstrate one's reputability, one supported conspicuous consumption, which was as lavish as one could make it, but not formless. In fact, the prescribed pecuniary canons of taste and dress, which required the conservation of archaic rituals and observances, were so difficult of mastery that they were specially assigned to the leisure class, which was mostly made up of women. Under a veneer of quasi-scientific objectivity, Veblen plainly despised what he analyzed, and contrasted pecuniary emulation with the instinct of workmanship. "[T]he end of vicarious consumption," he wrote, "is to enhance, not the fulness of life of the consumer, but the pecuniary repute of the master for whose behoof the consumption takes place."

That much of the world runs as Veblen described—though perhaps less now than a century ago—and that what he described was deserving of his scorn there is no doubt. Nevertheless, his analysis left consumption essentially outside of the economic process. It was the end—in the sense of terminus—of economic activity, but it was an unworthy end of unworthy activity. The contrasting instinct of workmanship perhaps led, in some not fully explained way, to fullness of life, but the enjoyment of this presumed fullness was a private affair—a result perfectly congenial to one of Veblen's reclusive temperament.

Consequently it remains that "the very idea of consumption itself has to be set back into the social process," as Mary Douglas and Baron Isherwood say in their book *The World of Goods*. These writers are concerned with "an anthropology of consumption," but their analysis opens the way for economic theory. They point out that in the history of anthropology "enlightenment has followed a decision to ignore the physiological levels of existence which sustain the behavior in question." Darwin had made a similar observation. "With plants," he exclaims in *The Origin of Species*, "how remarkable it is that the organs of vegetation, on which their nutrition and life depend, are of little significance [for

classification]!" Accordingly Douglas and Isherwood see consumption not as sustaining life but as "the joint production,
with fellow consumers, of a universe of values. Consumption
uses goods to make firm and visible a particular set of judgments in the fluid process of classifying persons and events."

The universe of values does not exist except in the process
of becoming firm and visible. Consumption is a form of communication. By what I spend my money on—the clothes I
wear, the food I eat, the furniture, books, and pictures with
which I surround myself—I discover and refine the standards to which I repair and thereby demonstrate to others
the sort of person I am, the sort of people with whom I
associate and whose good opinion and good fellowship I
value. As with other forms of communication, we are dealing
here, not with means, but with structure.

The anthropologist discovers and describes the structures
as they appear in the world of the Trobriand Islanders or in
the world of American business leaders. The economist must
either pass judgment on these structures or, as we have said,
he must acknowledge that his discipline is irrelevant to public policy.

The problem of judging consumption is not different from
the problem of judging production. In neither case does one
face the problem as a newborn babe or from behind a veil or
blindfolded. One is in the midst of one's life, of one's society, of one's times, of one's history, and one does not exist
otherwise. No solution will be valid that stunts one's life or
damages one's fellows or disregards the situation in which
one finds oneself or forgets what the past has left unsolved.
In considering these questions, we are back, as always, to
self-assertion.

I am the judge of my purposes, but I am not the only
judge. If my actions are unworthy, it is my soul that is
shriveled. I pay the price and have my reward. But society
also has an interest in what I do and is my judge because I
am literally nothing if not social. All of this works both ways.
Individual and society are symbiotic, reciprocal, mutually
necessary, ontological. Society is literally nothing except as a

membership of individuals, and this fact lays upon me the right and requirement to judge society. If a society's actions are unworthy, all the citizens suffer. All Americans were diminished by the Vietnam War; all are diminished by economic policies that condemn fellow citizens to lives of desperate poverty; all are diminished by the persistence of unjust laws.

9

CAPITAL

Why England Is Not Spain

The goods we have been discussing are consumers' goods—things and services to be used and enjoyed. Their role in the economy is systematically different from that of producers' goods—things and services to make consumers' goods or other producers' goods. Producers' goods exist in every system, no matter how primitive or advanced. The first producers' goods were no doubt clubs to attack game, or stones to crack shells. Puny humans would barely survive without such goods, but with them they perform miracles. The miraculous properties of producers' goods were not quickly recognized and consequently for a long time—until the sixteenth century—were not fully exploited.

The discovery of the sixteenth century was, as Keynes put it, the discovery (or perhaps rediscovery) of compound interest. He once calculated that every £1 that Sir Francis Drake plundered from Spain and brought home in 1580 had become £100,000 by 1930, and that the total was equivalent to the entire overseas wealth of the British Empire at its height. Looking ahead, he indulged the hope that the same process would solve "the economic problem" in another hundred years or so (more than fifty of which have already gone by) and that economists would then be "thought of as humble competent people, on a level with dentists."

While awaiting that happy day, we should notice that in

103

speaking of compound interest Keynes was not speaking as bankers speak in soliciting our deposits. He was not speaking of money but of producers' goods bought with Drake's gold and silver, and of the progressive investment and reinvestment of a part of the proceeds of those goods in further producers' goods, and so on, for 350 years. The reinvestments were small, averaging about 3¼ percent a year; but the results were stupendous. Spain, in contrast, though her plunder from the Americas was vastly greater than Drake's plunder from her, used practically all of her gold and silver to pay for consumers' goods, from castles in Iberia to armies in Italy and the Low Countries, with results that left her far in the British wake. Money, in short, is not a producers' good, any more than it is a consumers' good. Money can buy either kind of goods, but it is not, in itself, either kind.

Just as there is nothing inherent in an object that makes it a good, there is nothing inherent in a good that makes it a producers' good. A hammer may be used in producing something for sale, in which case it is a producers' good. Or it may be used about the house or even become an object for collectors, in which cases it is a consumers' good. At another time, a harried collector may grab it to drive a nail into something he intends to sell; then it becomes a producers' good again. A hen is a producers' good if her eggs are sold, but she herself may be literally consumed and so lay no more eggs. Even a steel mill may become a consumers' good; one near Völklingen in the Saar sheltered displaced persons for a time after World War II.

These classifications seem to reduce the real world to one of shifting and contradictory appearances. A hammer would seem to be both a consumers' good and not a consumers' good, which is logically impossible. But the object in question is not even a hammer in its qualities, or even in its shape (it might be a gavel), but in its use. The hammer is neither producers' goods nor consumers' goods—nor goods at all—except in the way it is used.

ii

In the official government National Product Accounts, a new single-family dwelling counts as a capital investment, no matter who pays for it or how anyone uses it. Some writers justify this sort of classification on the ground of the durability of the house. But durability is an uncertain test: I have many books that are older than any house I have ever owned or lived in. The Chicago school of economists goes still further afield, and Professor Friedman has classified consumer durables and even clothing as "savings." It is true that my dinner jacket has outlasted seven or eight automobiles and, given the amount of wear it gets, can outlast seven or eight more. It is also true that it cost me less when I bought it than a replacement would cost me today, but this differential is savings only in the huckster's sense of "Sale! Up to 50% Savings!" I did not buy it for any productive purpose. Nor did I buy it for a speculative purpose; and I'd have been disappointed if I had, for in the absence of an established market for secondhand clothes, the cost of selling it would have eaten up the putative "profit." On the other hand, if I were a headwaiter, the dinner jacket might be a necessary uniform and so productive.

The danger in all nonfunctional classifications quickly appears when we look again at the question of compound interest. Castles in Spain were big-ticket items and durable, and the grandees who built them saved or borrowed money for the purpose. But the castles were consumers' goods; they were not used to produce anything except plunder and extortionate rents, both of which are, literally, counterproductive. In contrast, the British steadily ploughed 3¼ percent of their earnings back into the shops for which Napoleon scorned them, and into mines and railways and factories and ships, all of which, in turn, produced further goods. The Spanish investments satisfied the durability definition; the British investments satisfied functional definitions. There is a practical difference.

We must not conclude, however, that there is a standard

percentage of income that an economy should invest, year in and year out. Here again it proves impossible to avoid passing judgment. The 3¼ percent rate of British imperialism may for some purposes have been too high, for others too low, though we can be pretty sure that it was more suitable than the near-zero Spanish rate. Nor is the classification of residential housing as investment likely to result in misdirection of public expenditure today, when so many live in substandard conditions.

It is in studies of the distribution of wealth that the faulty classification is misleading. As Lester Thurow points out, "Standard economics . . . assumes that people accumulate wealth solely to provide future consumption privileges," but great wealth results in economic power, "which entails the ability to order others about." Most Americans have little or no net wealth, and even the middle class have most of their wealth in the form of their homes. Since the recent inflation has greatly increased the value of residential housing, the distribution of wealth seems more equitable than formerly. But home ownership conveys no economic power, and Thurow shows that about 40 percent of all fixed nonresidential capital is controlled by only 482 families and individuals. Thus very few can order very many about.

iii

The modern mode of production differs from previous modes not in that it uses or exploits producers' goods (for all modes do that), nor in that it uses or exploits labor (for all modes also do that), but in that it is organized as a system of continuous and interrelated flows. Such retail trade as existed in Aristotle's time was frowned on by him because he could not see how a retailer produced anything. In the ancient and medieval worlds, enterprises were relatively discrete and *ad hoc* affairs, as the construction industry is largely organized to this day. If one wanted a pair of shoes, one went to a cordwainer and had a pair custom made; there was no store in which one could buy what one wanted off the shelf.

The cordwainer, to be sure, was a specialist in leather working, and the apprentices he employed were, so to say, subspecialists, one perhaps being more skilled at preparing the leather, another at sewing. The efficiency of the division of labor had, as we have noted, been early remarked by Plato; it, too, fails to mark the modern mode.

What was true of small transactions was true of large. The merchants of Venice organized each commercial voyage as a separate affair. Their personal experience taught them the sorts of goods most likely to be wanted on the Golden Horn, and they stocked their outward-bound galleys accordingly. Likewise they brought home the sorts of things they could sell quickly and profitably at the quayside. The system was a series of speculative ventures, making the most of *ad hoc* opportunities to buy and sell. Those involved were, as they called themselves, merchant adventurers.

Modern economy, in contrast, is a flow. The first modern business was probably the wool trade, a trade that peculiarly lent itself to such organization. In the first place, the wool itself was, comparatively, not perishable. At all stages—as raw wool, as yarn, as cloth—it could be fairly safely stockpiled; working capital was born. Each stage, moreover, required a special machine—a spinning wheel, a loom: fixed capital. The entrepreneur bought wool from the farmers, put it out for spinning and weaving, generally on his own looms, gathered the finished cloth, and held it for sale to merchant adventurers, or sometimes handled the distribution himself in an early form of vertical monopoly. The flow could be steady because the end product—clothing—was in universal and perpetual demand.

Yet no one knew, when the sheep were sheared, what would ultimately become of the wool, nor could the entrepreneur be perfectly sure he would find a ready market, at a price to cover his costs, when he collected the finished cloth from his weavers. But the rationale of his enterprise required him to keep going. With flowing enterprise came increased uncertainty. The medieval or Renaissance guild master manufactured his products to order, reducing uncertainty to a minimum. There are two sides to uncertainty: one

is risk, and the other is opportunity, and they contract or
expand together.

iv

Whether enterprise is flowing or relatively static, the producers' goods used therein are things that have been saved.
Agriculture is impossible unless seeds are set aside, reducing
current consumption to ensure future consumption. In addition, labor must be devoted to making tools, building fences,
turning pots for storage; and all these activities reduce the
time available for idleness, recreation, and other forms of
current consumption. Everyone is familiar with the story of
the ant and the grasshopper and with the history of the suffering in Jamestown due to the unmotivated idleness of gentlemen and the unmitigated slothfulness of servants. In an
industrial society, it is plain that power looms produce more
cloth per man hour than hand looms, and that power looms
are bought by men who have saved money or can borrow
money from others who have saved.

But the fact is that saving is a consequence of production.
Keynes called it a mere residual. This is no paradox. No
good can be saved until it exists. No good exists until it has
been produced. Production is inescapably prior to saving.
Even the standard agricultural model fails: seed corn cannot
be saved unless it has already been harvested.

In a modern economy, the priority of production is even
more striking. When a corporation plans a new product, contracts are entered into with a construction company to build
a factory, with tool manufacturers for the necessary machines, perhaps with an advertising agency for marketing
plans, and so on. The corporation also assures itself of a line
of credit to meet payments on these contracts as they come
due. The bank that grants the line of credit gets its affairs in
order so that it can do what it has agreed to do. The various
contractors and subcontractors and their banks all go through
the same motions. Aside from a down payment here and
there, no money is paid over until quite a lot of time has

passed and quite a lot of work has been done. In short, a great expansion of credit takes place, including that extended by the workers (who customarily wait a week or a month for their pay), that extended by merchants satisfying the demands of the newly employed workers, that extended by wholesalers and manufacturers restocking the merchants, and so on, via what R. F. Kahn called the multiplier.

The expansion of credit comes about, not as a result of savings, but as a result of production put in process by the corporation. These plans, to be sure, could have been aborted if the bank had not extended the line of credit, and so some may be tempted to think the production dependent upon the bank's assets, which are somebody's savings. Even with fractional-reserve banking, some may say, a bank must have *some* assets before it creates money by extending credit. Yet this is merely a consequence of current laws and customs. The reserve might be anything between zero and 100 percent (or even more) without affecting the principle involved. The new credit is money regardless of the size of the reserve.

Furthermore, no amount of savings by bankers and potential workers and suppliers would, in itself, have called the new production into existence. Nothing would have been produced if the enterprising corporation had not decided it could make a profit on it and if the people and firms it dealt with had not had faith in its ability to do it.

v

Profit is the economic reward of enterprise, as wages are the reward of labor, interest the reward of lending money, rent (if it still be a usefully distinct factor) the reward of lending land or utilities in the broadest sense. Enterprise was formerly an individual and personal affair, and still is to some extent, but is now mainly the work of corporations, whose legal owners take no responsibility for the business, and whose active managers are salaried employees. Profit, whether personal or corporate, is what is left after all expenses have been paid. This simple definition will bear close attention, both for what it says and for what it does not say.

What this definition says is that profit is something other than wages, interest, or rent. It does not say that profit has any analyzable cause or any assignable amount. It is merely what is left after the products of the enterprise have been sold and its expenses paid.

Profit is systematically different from interest, though they are often confused. Interest is money paid according to contract for the present use of money. Profit is the uncertain return of enterprise—that is, of making or doing something. When an entrepreneur provides his own money (or when a firm finances this year's expansion out of last year's profits), it may happen that an explicit charge is not made for the use of the money. It may also happen that an entrepreneur does not charge the enterprise for personal services rendered. In these situations, wages as well as interest become commingled with profits, to the possible confusion of the taxing authorities, and to the great confusion of legislators and judges trying to understand how the economy works, and how it should work.

Enterprise always has something left over—it may be loss or it may be gain—because the future is unknown and unknowable. No matter how carefully we plan, we must, in the end, be more or less surprised. This is not merely a statistical result, as is the fact that half of the parties to a gamble must be disappointed. Nor is it merely an empirical observation of the outcomes of the best-laid plans of mice and men. More important than statistics or empiricism, the systematic uncertainty of the future is a requirement of responsible assertion. If Pandora's box had not kept the future hidden, the present, too, would have been foreordained; life would have been a walking shadow; and there would not even have been a meaningful way of claiming that it was meaningless.

Insisting that something is always left over, we do not have to—indeed, we cannot—know where that something comes from. Our definition posits no specific source for profit. In some cases it may be the result of chance or a risk well run; in others the chance falls the other way. Sometimes it is the consequence (which for some enterprises may be favorable) of war or pestilence. Sometimes innovation is richly rewarded, and sometimes it is cruelly punished. Sometimes vigor achieves wonders; other times what was hoped to be vigorous action proves to have been the rushing in of fools. Whatever we may decide, after the fact, to have been the source of a particular profit, an enterprise has no way of systematizing all sources of future profits and losses. Whatever is systematically accounted for is thereupon allocated and charged to wages, interest, or rent. Profit or loss will still be left over.

vi

Economists nevertheless speak of "normal profit." Entrepreneurs, whether individual or corporate, will not ordinarily undertake a project unless they foresee such a normal profit, which is not a fixed rate but varies from industry to industry and from time to time. The normal profit will understandably bear some relationship to the interest rate the enterprise might otherwise earn with its money. This relationship is what is called an opportunity cost of the project. The enterprise evidently has the opportunity of earning at least that much by lending its money to someone else. The someone else would then have the trouble of doing something to cover the interest expense, and would run the risk of not being able to cover it. Since interest on a loan is a contract enforceable at law, the lender would save trouble and narrow risks by letting someone else do the work. With these factors in mind, entrepreneurs, depending on their confidence in their estimates of sales and expenses and on their enthusiasm for the project, set their normal profit, which is the minimum profit they must anticipate before undertaking a given work.

From the foregoing it will be recognized that the idea of a normal profit is useful, perhaps essential, in business planning, but that it does not affect the analysis of the source of profits, which are, in any enterprise, planned or actual, simply what is left over.

10

SPECULATION

Why Economics Is Not a Zero-Sum Game

i

So far we have assumed economic activity to be productive of goods—things or services bought and so consumed by people. But a substantial amount of activity—most, in fact, of what is called business by the newspapers—produces nothing whatever. Accounts of the doings on Wall Street are regularly presented on television programs as business reports; yet no discernible goods result from this busy-ness. There is, nevertheless, little doubt that the various stock and bond and commodities exchanges have enormous effects on the economy, both in detail and as a whole.

The trading on the exchanges concerns not things but what are called placements. Placements represent things, but usually no thing in particular. A stock certificate represents an undifferentiated share in the assets of a company; a bond represents a debt of the company; a commodities contract represents present or future ownership of some homogenous good like silver or wheat. Those who buy and sell placements—with the exception of those holding bonds to maturity—have no intention of ever laying their hands on what the placements represent, and generally they have no right to do so. A share of General Motors stock does not entitle one to turn it in for, say, a new tire or a set of wrenches.

Placements represent nothing in particular and sometimes nothing at all. A bankrupt firm has no net assets, and so its shares are shares of nothing. Commodities traders may buy and sell hog-belly futures—that is, contracts to deliver or acquire so many hog bellies at a specified future date at a specified price—without knowing whether that many hog bellies will be in existence at that date, or even having a very clear idea of what a hog belly is or why anyone would want one. The trader who sells for future delivery merely guesses that when the future comes the going price on that day will be lower than the price specified in his contract; he will then buy at the new price a contract to satisfy the buyer of his original contract, and pocket the difference. Of course, he may be caught short and so have to pay more than he got for his original contract, in which case he has a loss. It is a recurrent dream of traders to corner the market and catch everyone short. This is done by surreptitiously buying more of something—shares of stock or commodities—than actually exists; those who have contracted to sell must then frantically bid up the price to a level that satisfies the cornerer's killer instinct. For one reason or another, corners almost never succeed, though many buyers and sellers are ruined in the process.

Markets for placements must be made; that is, there must be traders always ready to buy or sell at bid and asked prices they publicly set. Where such markets do not exist, trading is sluggish and expensive, and the placements, whatever they may be, are less likely to be traded by people uninterested in the underlying goods.

ii

Trading in placements is speculation, for which we will give a special and precise definition. In ordinary speech, speculation tends to be defined somewhere between gambling and enterprise on a scale of relative riskiness. But betting on dice (which everyone would classify as gambling) is liable to risks that may be closely anticipated, while launching a new product (the quintessential example of productive enterprise) is likely to be very risky indeed. In the publishing business, most new books lose money, though this is not the deliberate intent of either authors or publishers. If no one takes risks of the latter sort, nothing is done; there is no economy to analyze. Riskiness is a tangle, not a continuum.

Instead of relative riskiness, the following criteria are proposed: *Gambling* is risking wealth in a truly zero-sum game. If some players win, some other players must lose the same amount. The winnings and losings (after properly allocating taxes and the house's cut) add up to zero.* *Speculation* differs from gambling in that it is not a zero-sum game. It can happen that all speculators win (though some may win more than others), that all lose, or that some win while others lose, and the sum of the winnings may be quite different from the sum of the losings. Speculation is, nevertheless, like gambling in that it produces nothing but rearranges— often to the great profit of the rearrangers—wealth that already exists. *Enterprise* is unlike speculation in that it uses wealth to produce new wealth, but it is alike in that it is not a zero-sum game. (If it were, it would be impossible for the economy to grow.) In a healthy economy it is possible for all reasonably astute producers to profit, at least to a degree. Prosperity in one business does not have to be counterbalanced by depression in some other; on the contrary, prosperity tends to spread.

On the basis of these definitions, gambling is, as is generally agreed, of negligible economic significance. It distracts some people from work of more evident usefulness but apparently provides them with amusement, which is a good. Its direct effects on the income or wealth of society are minimal.

Keynes made a small fortune for himself and enhanced a substantial endowment for King's College by speculating,

---

*Lester Thurow's *The Zero-Sum Economy* is mistaken in calling all sports—and by extension all social and economic activities—zero-sum games. Sports have winners and losers, but there is no sport in which the scores add up to zero.

mainly in foreign currencies and commodities. Commenting on these speculations, his biographer Roy Harrod writes: "As regards the gains of the successful speculator, in the case of the foreign exchanges, this was solely at the expense of the unsuccessful, who, since he had voluntarily incurred the risk, had no legitimate hardship if the risk went wrong. In the case of commodities, the same argument largely applied: what speculator A gained, speculator B lost."

Keynes himself came to have doubts about the innocence of speculation and attempted to distinguish it from enterprise by defining the former as "the activity of forecasting the psychology of the market," while the latter was "the activity of forecasting the prospective yield of assets over their whole life." There is no doubt that he disapproved of the former. He speaks of "the long-term investor . . . who most promotes the public interest"; and he proposes "the introduction of a substantial Government transfer tax . . . with a view to mitigating the dominance of speculation over enterprise in the United States." He does not, however, explain why this dominance is to be deplored. The most he says is that "When the capital development of a country becomes the by-product of a casino, the job is likely to be ill-done." His objection seems almost one of sophisticated distaste.

Very likely no stronger objection can be sustained so long as Keynes's definitions of speculation and enterprise are used. Forecasts are in the nature of things uncertain, and any benefits the economy might gain from them are uncertain. Keynes grants that a speculator may make more money than a long-term investor; and there seems no reason in principle why the "by-products" should necessarily differ.

iii

If, however, the stock exchange is not a "casino" (which does run zero-sum games), if it is instead an open-ended game, then substantive objections to speculation appear. In order to see more clearly what these may be, we may consider the distinction that Keynes makes between old investment and new investment, which latter he defines as "The increment of capital equipment, whether it consists of fixed capital, working capital or liquid capital." This definition fits very comfortably with the one we have given for enterprise; and what Keynes calls old investment (or buying and selling "secondhand" stocks or other financial instruments) fits with what we have called speculation.

The most obvious point is that without new investment there is no new enterprise, nor even much continuing enterprise, while what Keynes calls exchanges of old investments have no necessary effect on the enterprises that gave rise to them. It is not denied that there may be indirect effects, as in events like the Bendix fiasco of 1982 or in the way (probably exaggerated) in which the existence of a market for old investments may encourage the purchase of truly new issues. But the direct and ordinary effects are nil. It ordinarily makes no difference to an enterprise whether its stockholders are short term or long term, wise or foolish, gentlemen or riffraff. Nor does an enterprise ordinarily profit or lose from fluctuations in the market price of its securities. Even though a rising price may make further financing easier to arrange and may also enhance the prestige and salaries of the firm's executives, the firm itself gets its money from the initial sale of the securities and is thereafter relatively indifferent to what happens to the securities as old investments.

Speculation is of course not confined to the exchange of securities. It merely involves buying for eventual resale at a hoped-for higher price and thus also includes collecting exotic beer cans or old masters, hoarding gold pesos, and sitting on tracts of land. It also includes selling short. It is safe to say that practically the entire activity of the stock exchanges and commodities markets is devoted to speculation. There seem to be no statistics available on the proportion of exchange activity that concerns new investments; but even counting all new stock issues (and most of these merely refund old investments), it appears that the proportion is well under 1 percent. This speculative bias is likewise true of what preens itself as investment banking. Taking it all to-gether—stock exchanges, commodities markets, and invest-ment banking—this business is very large. It is probably what President Coolidge had in mind when he said, "The business of America is business."

Of these exchanges of old investments, Keynes says that they "necessarily cancel out." This conclusion seems ob-vious, for by definition no new thing is involved; so whatever old thing someone buys, someone else has to sell. At any given moment, therefore, the exchanges do certainly cancel out. But the economy is not static, and the markets are not static, and something makes the exchanges worth the bother in the actual situation. That something is money. Though no new thing is involved, the general level of the stock ex-change and the general level of the commodities, collect-ibles, and real-estate markets can rise, because additional money goes into speculation. Because of money, exchanging old investments is not a zero-sum game.

iv

This conclusion is questioned by many economists because the influx of money into the market has an effect only on the money prices of the old investments; it does not change their "real" value. Suffice it to say here that speculators act, and must act, on the basis of money prices in the same way and for the same reasons that, as Keynes showed, workers act on the basis of money wages rather than "real" wages. Whatever real prices and wages may be imagined to be, one will be better off with high money income than with low.

The insistence on "real" values is another form of the com-mon contention that speculation doesn't matter because it must all come to bricks and mortar or consumption in the end. Speculators, it is said, must do something with their winnings; they can't keep speculating forever. But of course they can—and do. Wall Street is thickly populated with individuals and firms that would think it improper to risk funds on a "new" investment. And given the fact that a new investment becomes "old" the first time it is traded, there cannot possibly be enough new investments to go around if there is any volume in the trading at all.

There is another factor in the situation: historical time. It is conceivable that things may come to consumption or to enterprise in the long run, but here, as in so many situations, Keynes's witticism is pertinent: "In the long run we are all dead." It might even happen that when the speculative frenzy collapses, and all accounts are somehow balanced, formulae could be devised to make it appear that speculation had been—in the long run—a zero-sum game. If so, the same might be said for inflation: what goes up is likely to come down—in the long run. In the meantime, which may be a very long time—more than twenty years in the case of Holland's tulip mania, almost ten in the case of the Great Bull Market of the twenties—both speculation and inflation cause grievous damage to society and to most of the individuals who make it up.

v

Why should speculative frenzy get under way in the first place? Society certainly needs markets for old investments so that institutional endowments and pension and insurance funds can at least be suitably liquid, and also so that cultural objects, from fine furniture to old masters, can be valued and cherished. Yet these exchanges are not necessarily frenzied. What makes them become so?

The answer is usually given in psychological terms. Certain people are said by nature to be speculators (Keynes thought this true of Americans), and at times a speculative fever seems to grip the land. The fever may be related to sunspots or to fear of war or to satisfaction with election returns. Sunspots aside, it will be remembered that the market broke in September 1939, and that it usually rises after

an election, no matter who wins. Such fluctuations are trivial; something more substantial than whim is surely at work
in any sustained rise. An explanation will be found in a high
interest rate, a volatile interest rate, or of course a combina-
tion of both.

A high interest rate is merely one higher than the ordinary
return an ordinarily successful firm can make on its equity;
that is, it is higher than what businessmen think of as their
normal profit. A relatively high rate will immediately discourage investment in new enterprise and will quickly discourage continuing investment in existing enterprise. Why
should I borrow to expand—or merely to maintain—my
business if the rewards of my effort go to my friendly
banker? Why should my banker lend me the money I need
to keep going if he can earn more, with less effort, by helping Chilean generals repress their people, or U.S. Steel to
take over Marathon Oil, or Bendix to make a mess of three
corporations in a pointless power struggle? The effects of a
high interest rate are thus what we might expect. Money is
diverted from enterprise to speculation. In at least the
United States and Great Britain, this diversion is accelerated
by special low taxation of capital gains. When the maximum
tax on a speculation is 20 percent, while the tax on enterprise is roughly 50 percent, anyone who works for a living
must be a workaholic. What is touted as a spur to enterprise
is instead a spur to speculation.

Obsessed by fear of inflation, the Federal Reserve Board
managed in 1951 to free itself from its wartime agreement
with the Treasury to hold interest rates down. Thereafter it
made spasmodic attempts to control inflation by inflating the
rate; and in the late 1970s decided to worry about the money
supply and allow the interest rate to soar erratically of its
own accord. There is no doubt that the policy was designed
to do what it did do: dampen enterprise, throw people out of
work, intimidate labor unions, and thus moderate the
money-wage aspect of inflation. A virtue was imagined
where a rational and compassionate man would see a vice.
Discussing the crash of 1929, Keynes wrote, "A rate of inter-

est, high enough to overcome the speculative excitement, would have checked, at the same time, every kind of reasonable new investment." This is what happened fifty years later.

Not only does speculation survive in conditions that dampen enterprise, it actually thrives in such conditions. Speculation, which depends on rising prices, is itself a stimulant to price rises. A rising commodities market necessarily forces up the prices of goods made from the commodities. A rising interest rate requires price rises to pay the bankers' bills. A rising interest rate therefore fuels the inflation it was supposed to dampen. Thus the immediate effect of the 1979 decision to encourage the interest rate to surge was a simultaneous surge of inflation. It took four years of depression and all the suffering that that entailed to bring inflation down to a rate that, being the lowest in ten years, elicited much self-congratulation but was actually substantially higher than the trend of the decades before the Federal Reserve Board began to worry about the money supply.

vi

Though it is a perversion of sound public policy to encourage speculation, it is nevertheless true that some sort of speculation is inevitable and even useful in our world of uncertainty.

Being unable to foretell the future, a business firm necessarily speculates when it orders capital goods for future delivery. When the goods come in, they may be worth more— or less—than the contract price, and the firm will accordingly realize a speculative profit or loss. To minimize such swings, a firm will sometimes hedge by speculating in placements—stocks, commodities, whatever. Thus, if the firm fears the delivered goods may turn out to be less valuable than the current price, it will sell placements short. Then, if prices fall, the money gained by the short-selling will offset the money lost on the capital goods. Of course, if inflation is anticipated, the buyer of capital goods is unlikely to hedge against that; but then the seller may hedge by hoping that an increase in the price of the placements he buys will offset increased costs of manufacturing the capital goods he sells.

It should be added that hedging, in spite of its occasional usefulness in helping individual firms to moderate profit swings, has little or no effect on the prices firms charge and consequently little or no effect on the price level. On the other hand, by increasing the amount of money devoted to speculation, hedging participates in the general deleterious effect on the economy. This participation is true also of such operations as Keynes's speculations in foreign currencies and also of collections of art and artifacts (also indulged in by Keynes), whose prices are supported in large part by the expectation that they can eventually be sold or even given away at a handsome profit underwritten by misguided provisions of the capital-gains tax and the charity deduction.

Wherever the monetary authorities attempt direct control of the money supply, speculation will drain money from both production and consumption. Wherever the monetary authorities encourage a high interest rate, speculation will be encouraged and enterprise will suffer. Wherever the monetary authorities allow loans to support margin trading on the exchanges, speculation will be encouraged and enterprise will suffer. Wherever the taxing authorities give favored treatment to capital gains, speculation will again be encouraged, and enterprise will again suffer.

It would be foolish to try to prevent speculation, not because people are psychologically addicted to it, but because the uncertainty of our lives makes it inevitable. At the same time, it is foolish to encourage it, as is almost universally done.

11

PROPERTY

The Labor Theory of Right

i

Since profits result from enterprise, profits should go to enterprise. As all modern economies have developed, however, profits accrue to capital, which is only one of the factors of enterprise. This is obviously true of capitalism, and it is true of communism as well, where the means of production, which is another name for capital, are the property of the state, not of the enterprises that do the producing.

It is easy to understand how this arrangement came about. Until very recently, all enterprises were conducted by individuals or small groups of individuals who had, in one way or another, amassed the wealth used in their businesses. Whatever land they used was also owned by them. And they themselves directed the enterprises and in many cases performed all the work involved. Consequently it was reasonable for the profits to go exclusively to them; and when it was a question of selling the business, the decision was theirs and the rewards were theirs. Today, however, though individual enterprises in the classic manner are large in numbers, they do a small proportion of the business of the country, reap a minuscule share of the profits, employ a tiny minority of the workers, are typically not in manufacturing, and generally have short and erratic lives. Makers of better mousetraps are largely figments of nineteenth-century romantic imagination.

The modern corporation is itself the entrepreneur. It may have started as a one-man show, and it may continue under the dominance of one man, who may be handsomely rewarded for his efforts. But it is a public corporation. He does not own it, and the profits go to those who do. The owners, moreover, and only they, have the right to sell the corporation or any part of it and to take for themselves the entire net proceeds of the sale. This is an anomalous state of affairs, because, as everyone knows, the legal owners of a modern corporation have practically nothing to do with it. The legal fiction has it that the stockholders elect the directors, and that the directors appoint and oversee the officers who conduct the daily business of the corporation. In practice, however, the officers select and dominate the directors, who are routinely elected by those stockholders who bother to return their proxies.

Not only do the stockholders have practically nothing to do with the corporation, they never wanted to have anything to do with it. They merely wanted to make a placement. They had somehow come into some money, and they wanted to place it where it would be reasonably liquid and also have a chance of returning something more than bank interest. The invention of the limited liability company was a blessing for such people, and the blessing was magnified by the creation of efficient securities markets. Since, with negligible exceptions, shares are "fully paid and nonassessable," those who hold them need not worry about the company's debts, nor need they fear the loss, even in the extreme case, of more than they paid for the stock. And since they can sell out at any time, they need not fuss about providing alternatives to company policies they find unsatisfactory. Instead of trying to organize opposing points of view, they can sell out and register their meaningless disapproval in that way.

No matter what careless or even deliberate horror is perpetrated by their company, the owners accept no responsibility. They would not, they insist, have become owners if responsibility had been expected of them. How could they have known that the gasoline tank of the Pinto was unsafely designed? How could they have known that DES might cause cancer? How could they have known that exposure to asbestos could lead to leukemia twenty years later? And if there had been some way in which such knowledge could have been available to them, what could they as individuals, each with a few shares or even thousands of shares, have done about it? There was no way in which they could effectively participate in the daily operations of Ford or Lilly or Johns Manville; and on the other side, the managements of those companies would claim that they could not operate with such participation. Aside from the confusion that would result, what could then be done to protect trade secrets (whatever they may be)?

Etymologically, property is associated with proper—special, particular, distinctive, characteristic; peculiar, restricted; private, individual. A share of stock qualifies for none of these attributes; its virtue is that it does not. No one makes a claim to distinction on the basis of owning shares of a public company. One may boast of having made a killing in this stock or that, but what one calls attention to is one's cleverness, not its vehicle. In all this, shares of stock are similar to other placements, all of which are easily marketable and essentially anonymous. But only shares of stock assert the right to profits and, theoretically, to control.

ii

These rights are what the stockholders' property consists of. Property is not a thing but a bundle of rights. Rights may be attached to any object, but rights do not inhere in any object. No object has rights, because no object can fulfill duties. Not even the environment, so much and so properly talked of, has rights. If I am enjoined from polluting or destroying it, the society is what lays the injunction on me. Air, water, and other natural resources, by themselves, can do nothing to me or for me. I can use them, but the using is my doing, not theirs; and I use them carefully in my interest and in that of my fellow citizens. My fellow citizens have rights in the environment, but the environment itself has none. It is thus a confusion of terms to speak of property rights as opposed to human rights. Property has no rights; human beings may have property, which is the right to use a certain object in certain ways. In the other direction, I have no rights in human beings, but I do have rights in property.

Producers' goods, as we have said, are good and valuable through their participation in a system of production, which is related to a system of consumption, which, in turn, ratifies consumers' goods. This statement is, so far, neutral as to persons; it says nothing about the ownership of these goods. The personal ownership of consumers' goods presents no great problem; whoever consumes them thereby owns them. You can't possess the bread that I eat, and you have no desire to possess my toothbrush. I may be in debt to you for the cost of the bread or the toothbrush, but the bread and the toothbrush, themselves, are mine.

In general, there is no doubt that at least some consumers' goods can be personal property, though the rights may be limited or modified in various ways (for no right is absolute), and the limitations and modifications may change as the world changes. The great problems concern the ownership of producers' goods, because that ownership includes the right to control production. Since everyone is either a producer or dependent on a producer, those who own producers' goods have control of their fellows in a vital way.

The owners, though they do not renounce the control, are more interested in their income than in their property. An investment in shares of stock is legally different from purchase of a bond or a promissory note, but the earnings of both are generally justified in the same way. Dividends and interest are both said to be rewards of risk taking and abstinence. (Alfred Marshall preferred "waiting" to "abstinence" on the reasonable ground that rich people were not especially noted for the latter.) Neither stockholder nor bondholder does in fact do anything more for an enterprise than provide it with money; they are alike in this. Both stockholder and bondholder abstain from present enjoyment of their money; they are alike in this, too. They differ somewhat in the risks they run. If the enterprise fails, the stockholder usually loses all he invested, while the bondholder has a lien on the firm's assets and is able to salvage a few cents on the dollar. To balance the difference in risks, the bondholder's remuneration is limited to a fixed rate of interest, while the stockholder will prosper in proportion to the prosperity of the enterprise.

Abstinence, however, is not the exclusive province of stockholders and bondholders. The workers' abstinence is no less severe; they stay on the job instead of going fishing or lying in the sun. Some workers may not absent themselves from felicity to the satisfaction of some observers. The same can be said of some holders of placements.

Nor is risk taking an exclusive function. Life is risky, and no life is more risky than that of the unendowed working man or woman. The stockholders' risk is obvious: they may lose their shirts and have to work to get another. The laborers' risk is no less real for being possibly less dramatic: they devote time and sometimes money to learning a skill that may become worthless if the enterprise fails. They are also more closely committed to the enterprise than are the stockholders or bondholders. It is more difficult for them to pull out at the first sign of faltering, for jobs are hardly ever easy to find, and they cannot handily move from town to town in search of work. The stockholders or bondholders have only to call their brokers. Finally, the workers may be ruined by the company's decision to move from one locality to another, while the stockholders may gain from such a shift.

iii

Whatever one owns came into existence—not as a mere object, but as an economic good—as a result of labor. Its production entailed the use of producers' goods, which in their turn are the result of labor. And it came into one's possession as a result of labor, whether one's own or someone else's.

Because labor, whether current labor or past labor, is the source of economic goods, many have attempted to find in labor the source of value. These attempts have failed, but the impulse behind them was sound. Labor is primary, though not the source of value. Instead, labor is the source of right.

What is here proposed is a Labor Theory of Right. It is by labor and only by labor that we produce goods and come to possess them. Producers' goods are not only labor-saving or labor-enhancing devices; they are themselves encapsulated labor or, as Marx called them, frozen labor. Nothing exists except in conjunction with human activity. Whatever is made is made by the hand of man—literally manufactured—and whatever services are performed are performed by men and women. Capital, no matter how defined otherwise, is saved labor.

Both current labor and saved or past labor are involved in the act of production, and so both are entitled to participate in the proceeds. The entitlement of current labor is immediate: the workers are present, and the sweat glistens on their brows. But the entitlement of the owners of capital is secondary: it depends on the fact that their capital was itself once a direct entitlement of labor. Thus their entitlement cannot rise higher than that of labor, which is its source. What is past, what is even dead and gone, cannot take precedence over what is now and is continuing. "*Owning* capital," as Joan Robinson said, "is not a productive activity."

The right of labor to participate in profit is bolstered by the implications of any employment contract. As we saw in the little hiring scenario in Chapter 5, it is in the nature of things necessary either for employers to pay their employees in advance, or for employees to do a job before they are paid for it. The latter option being the custom in our system, the employees of any business have their earnings for half a pay period on perpetually revolving interest-free loan to the business. In the case of an annual bonus, the period of the loan averages out to six months. As a result, the business can make a corresponding expansion of plant or inventory or marketing services. In short, its capital is increased by this contribution of labor as effectively as it is by the cash contributions of capitalists.

Thus there is no right that capitalists can claim that laborers do not have a claim to. If capitalists have a right to control enterprise, so do laborers. If capitalists have a right to receive profits—or suffer losses—so do laborers. In theory, the right of one is not stronger than the other's. A good society, however, will recognize the wisdom and justice of Jefferson's dictum: "Life is for the living."

iv

Rights exist only as they are asserted. No right exists merely because it is asserted, but no right exists unless it is asserted. The assertion of a right is an act of will, and the recognition of a right, as by law, is an act of will in which everyone participates as a member of society. The failure to assert a right is also an act of will, as is the failure to accept responsibility; and the failure of the law to assign a responsibility is a failure of the will of the society.

Il gran rifiuto of today's economic life is the stockholders' assertion, supported by the law, of ownership rights and their simultaneous refusal, also supported by the law, of all ownership duties whatever. Classical entrepreneurs were proud of their enterprises. They were textile manufacturers, dry-goods merchants, railroaders. No one claims that such commitment was or can be a certain preventive of abuses of all kinds—abuses of workers, of investors, of the public— but it does clear a ground of responsible action for those with the will to occupy it. But to be a conglomerate man is to be nobody in particular, with no commitment to anything in particular except the bottom line, the bottom line being in fact the only excuse for the conglomerate.

This is the triumph of finance over production, and it is

inexorable so long as ownership carries no responsibilities. Irresponsible owners can be interested only in money. They are classical economic men par excellence, and they will go where they can get the most of what they are interested in. They will consequently put pressure on brokers to find for them companies that will slake their thirst; brokers will pressure investment bankers to float the issues of such companies; investment bankers will pressure commercial bankers to give priority to such companies; and all pressure will be brought to bear on the management of every public company to do whatever needs to be done to increase the bottom line.

That frequently the easiest way to increase the bottom line is to go, as they say, the merger and acquisition and diversification route is only the most visible outcome. Such maneuvers generally can increase the bottom line only by "rationalizing" the merged companies—which means closing plants and firing people. In such circumstances, loyalty is comprehensively destroyed. No one is or can afford to be loyal to the enterprise—not the owners, not the financiers, not the management, not the work force. Nor are owners, financiers, managers, or workers encouraged to be loyal to each other. This atomization of concern is doubtless a major cause of the widely deplored decline in standards of workmanship. It certainly is a major cause of increased speculation on Wall Street.

It should be noted that the pressures we have mentioned come from stockholders and the brokers and other intermediaries between them and the corporation; they do not come from bondholders. This is not because bondholders are more decent people than stockholders (often they are the same), but because the bondholders' care about the bottom line is only that it be large enough for them to be confident of their regular interest payments and of the principal at maturity. This is a very relaxed care in comparison with the stockholders' frenzied search for profits. Although the bondholders' role is to provide the corporation with needed financing, bondholders have nothing to gain from financial wheeling and dealing; and such trading as they do turns on the general interest rate, not on the performance of the company issuing the bonds. Their interests are similar to the workers', except for those of the few managerial workers whose attention to speculators' interests enables them to construct golden parachutes from their present positions or golden rockets to better ones elsewhere.

The public consequences of atomization are matched by personal consequences whose severity cannot be over-emphasized. Loyalty is one of the fundamental virtues; Josiah Royce held it to be the fundamental virtue. Deprive men and women of the opportunity for loyalty, and you shrivel their souls. Encourage them to be disloyal, and you corrupt them. When such encouragement is pervasive, corruption is almost impossisble to reverse. Cynicism cannot cure itself; it must be surprised—happily by joy, unhappily by catastrophe. The damned are those who are not surprised at all.

None of this is necessary. It is a result of the faulty design of the modern corporation.

v

The irresponsibility of stockholders has been widely noted, and much legal ingenuity has been lavished on proposals to correct the situation. Some of these notions try in one way or another to make it easier for dissidents to be elected to the boards of directors, thus presumably encouraging stockholders to pay attention. Others would mandate representatives of "the public" on the boards, thus trying to make the boards responsible to somebody even if the stockholders are responsible to no one.

All such schemes are doomed to failure, not because they are necessarily wrong-headed, but because no one actually wants them. A few enthusiasts now busy themselves in attending and speaking up at stockholders' meetings, but investors with a prudently diversified portfolio could not possibly master the intricacies of the businesses they partly own. They realize they could not; so they sensibly find better things to do with their time. Public board members would not be in much better case. They could not expect to make a career attending board meetings, nor could they realistically expect to learn enough about any company to be useful. The most likely outcome is that they would be coopted by their genial colleagues; and if they should entertain ideas at variance with those of the rest of the board, they would find it difficult to overcome the pressures of small-group psychology, especially as the public to whom they were supposed to be responsible would not only be largely indifferent but would also have no way of supporting or rejecting the board members' ideas.

More important, the public's interest in any particular company is abstract and can be satisfied by general laws. The public is reasonably concerned that the corporation pay its taxes, abjure fraud, respect its workers, not harm the environment, and refrain from skittering hither and thither in search of weak laws and low taxes. These ends could and should be served by national legislation and are not likely to be served otherwise. There is, however, no rational possibility of framing a law requiring stockholders to assume any responsibility that they could not in practice discharge— one, moreover, that neither they nor the corporations they invest in want them to have.

Why, then, should stockholders, who refuse the duties of ownership, be protected in the rights of ownership? There is actually only one reason: They now enjoy those rights. Abstinence and risk taking they share with bondholders and employees; management they leave to a special kind of employee. What is left is possession, and that is nine points of the law.

The tenth point, however, is rationality, and movement should be in that direction. Although it is surely impossible to imagine the easy success of any movement to reform the modern corporation, it is not difficult to suggest points that such reform might encompass. Starting with the understand-

ing that the corporation is the entrepreneur and so entitled
to the profits and the capital gains, one would ask, Who are
the *people* of the corporation? And the answer would be that
they are first and foremost those who do the work of the
corporation, namely the management and the other workers,
and secondarily the stockholders, and that they all should be
able to share in both rewards and control. As a first approx-
imation of how these shares should be allocated, one might
assume that there is some rationality behind the present distribution. At present, management and other workers get
wages and bonuses and fringe benefits, and stockholders get
dividends, and these are the more or less satisfactory result
of explicit or implicit negotiations. Each individual's proper
share might then be determined by taking the individual's
income from the corporation, whether wages or dividends or
both, and dividing it by the total of all such incomes from
the corporation (not, certainly, counting interest). Cash dividends would be paid in accordance with such shares, which
would be recalculated annually.

In addition to cash dividends—and it is a crucial addition—new stock equal in value to the corporation's increase
in net worth would be issued in the same proportions as cash
dividends (or stock would be canceled if net worth fell). This
stock—and sooner or later all stock in the corporation—
would be inalienable. It could not be sold or bequeathed or
pledged as security for a loan or even given away; but it
could at any time be exchanged with the corporation for a
negotiable note or bond or, at the corporation's option, cash.
And such an exchange would *have* to be made when the
owner of the stock left the corporation, retired, was fired, or
died. Over the years—within a generation at the outside—
most of the present stockholders would be converted into
bondholders. They would have their reward. The remaining
stockholders would all be active in the business. They could,
of course, like their predecessors, run it well or ill, could sell
it or merge it or adandon it; but whatever happened, it
would be their doing, and they would be the ones to benefit
or suffer from it.

It is very likely that reform of corporate internal structure would have to be complemented by reform of external structure. Certainly all corporations, regardless of internal reform, should be nationally chartered and subject only to national taxation and regulation. Only in this way can one hope to overcome the states' temptations to play beggar my neighbor by luring companies away from each other with tax breaks and permissive regulation. Sooner or later, too, it will probably become apparent that antitrust laws should turn on size, not on competition—partly because the courts have proved incapable of defining competition without interminable and inconclusive litigation, partly because competition is by no means always beneficent, and partly because small is beautiful.

vi

In his book *Beauty Looks After Herself*, Eric Gill wrote that a slave does what he has to do when he is at work and what he wants to do on his own time, while a free man does what he wants to do when he is at work and what he has to do on his own time. On this basis, most men and women are slaves, though in bondage only to themselves. The reasons for this are various, and they are by no means all economic.

The economic reasons flow largely from the authoritarian and megalomaniac structure of most contemporary business enterprises. Small is indeed beautiful. This is not because small is more efficient than giantism. Maybe it is, and maybe it isn't. The beauty of smallness is in the eye of the producer, not necessarily of the consumer. A small company can be a better place to work than a large one. Small institutions can allow more scope for individual assertiveness and creativeness and responsibility of all kinds than large ones do. But there is no necessity about this. Her people and her institutions made Athens the school of Hellas, as Pericles said; the less-distinguished neighboring city-states were less remarkable but not because they were larger or smaller.

The beauty of smallness is that it diffuses power, not that it expands competition. Neither competition nor its mirror image, cooperation, is an end in itself. Competition is the sanitized descendant of Thomas Hobbes's war of all against all, and cooperation is the prudent alternative to that war.

Theory has it that competition spurs workers to greater productivity and entrepreneurs to cheaper and more plentiful products. Without this spur, it is said, the world would stumble, while with the spur the economy leaps from triumph to triumph—and not just the economy, because statesmen and artists and scholars compete for fame, as workers and entrepreneurs compete for money.

This is a pretty story, often told, and there is much truth in it; but it has an ugly side. Very early on, it was recognized that unregulated competition drives wages down to the subsistence level and keeps them there. The competition of entrepreneur against entrepreneur prevents even the tender hearted from paying more, while the competition of worker against worker prevents even the stout hearted from holding out for more. This is the Iron Law of Wages, which prompted Carlyle to call economics the dismal science.

Not only does competition have an ugly side; it also turns out to be diffuse and shapeless. One can, for example, read only so many suspense novels in a year; so a given suspense novel obviously competes with all the other suspense novels in print. But it also competes with true spy stories, with movies, with a TV on the installment plan, with other forms of entertainment, with forms of quasi-entertainment (like a new gadget for an automobile), and ultimately with everything on the market. In short, at any given moment, consumers have a limited number of dollars to spend, and what is spent on one thing cannot be spent on something else. This fact emboldens apologists for big business to argue that even oligopolies must operate in the market as if so-called perfect competition obtained. If automobile manufacturers tried to gouge consumers, it is explained, the latter would run their old cars a while longer and spend their money on something else.

There is some truth in this tale, too. But if everything competes with everything, there is no need to worry (as some, like Friedrich Hayek, do) about an end to the "competitive system." What exists anyhow, regardless of what anyone does, needs no defense and indeed admits of none. Consequently it is understandable that the courts have been unable to settle on a clear approach to antitrust law. A prime example of the absurdity of trying to use competition as a touchstone for the organization of business is the established legal principle that a company may engage in certain business practices otherwise defined as unfair if it can show it does so to meet competition.

Similar difficulties and absurdities would arise if cooperation were substituted as the touchstone. We are all interdependent and so cooperation is as universal as is competition; there is even honor among thieves. Courts devoted to the idea of cooperation would, in addition, be bewildered by the ancient common-law notion of conspiracy, particularly a conspiracy in restraint of trade.

Eventually we may come to see that our freedom depends on neither competition nor cooperation but on the control of size as such. Big can be ugly, especially when it is encouraged by the tax laws to engage in the sorts of speculation described in Chapter 10 and the neo-imperialism to be described in Chapter 14.

vii

The invisible hand was supposed to drive prices down and quality up. Professor Galbraith has taught us not to expect the market to work that way in the world of big business, which he calls the planning system. But it doesn't work as it is famed to do even in what he calls the market system.

In the textbook business, which is minutely fragmented and fiercely competitive, competition frequently has the effect of pushing prices up rather than down. As an apposite example, we may consider one of the biggest submarkets of the textbook market—the freshman principles of economics course. Forty years ago the texts for this course looked like ordinary books; you could hold them in one hand while you read them; and you could carry them to class without backache. Then one of the publishers got the idea of dressing up his entry with a second color, which would sometimes make the graphs a bit easier to understand and might make the whole thing look livelier. The second color would have approximately doubled the printing costs if the publisher had not dramatically increased his market share. The increased attractiveness increased sales, which permitted longer press runs, which helped hold the price down. But of course the other publishers quickly copied the innovation, with the result that each publisher soon had roughly the same market share as before. Press runs were necessarily reduced to those of pre-color days; so unit costs went up. As costs went up, so did prices. It cannot be pretended that students' understanding of economics has improved proportionately.

Such a competitive dance is performed in many another industry, forcing prices up rather than down, reducing the variety of goods offered for sale, and generally (as a book of business advice once had it) selling the sizzle rather than the steak. This outcome is a puzzle to classical economists, but it can be readily explained. The explanation does not, I hasten to add, turn on the slyness of the competitors, who are no worse and no better than anyone else.

The explanation does turn on one or two facts about the industries involved. The so-called law of supply and demand will not work in its classical way in those industries in which either the supply or the demand is systematically limited or, as economists say, inelastic. In the textbook business, for example, it is the demand that is limited. There are only so many students taking freshman economics in any given year; so there is nothing any publisher can do to make much difference in the size of the market. Students who have one textbook have no use for another at any price. The students, moreover, themselves have limited options. Assuming that they're going to study at all, they can buy a new copy of the textbook, or they can buy a secondhand copy, or they can borrow their roommate's copy. They do not have the option of substituting something else. If the assigned text is Mansfield's, they can hardly make do with Samuelson's, and they certainly can't substitute *The Norton Anthology of English Literature*, no matter how great a bargain it is.

Faced with this limited market, publishers have correspondingly limited options. If they want a larger share of the market, they can seek it by lowering their price or "upgrading" their product, or both. A little business experience will convince them that price lowering, by itself, is seldom the solution of choice. Henry Ford almost ruined his company by sticking doggedly with his Model T long after Chevrolet had come out with a somewhat more practical, more comfortable, and vastly more stylish competitor at a considerably higher price. At the other end of the business scale, restaurants find it profitable to serve extra-large portions at extra-large prices. The gourmands among their customers will happily eat what's put before them, and the gourmets will be delighted to take home a doggy bag full of expensive morsels for their pets (or for their own next-day's supper). In all these instances, producers have found again and again that while price may be a factor, it is by no means the most significant factor in the competition for market shares.

A limited supply will similarly upset the classical theory that competition invariably benefits consumers. In spite of the frenzy of the fall of 1983, there was not, it turned out, a substantial shortage of Cabbage Patch dolls. Competition forced retailers to bid the price up in order to get something to draw customers into their stores; consequently a little shortage became, as a result of competition, a temporarily big one. Something like this happens almost every Christmas without hurting anyone very much. (There is one case in which almost everyone is hurt, and seriously, and that is the case of banking, which is worth a chapter to itself.)

The failure of competition to perform as theory says it does is no surprise to anyone, not even to classical economists. Examples of the failure are too many and too obvious, but they are blandly swept under the rug with the proposition that the public gets what it demands. No one really believes that, and the proposition cannot be proved or disproved on its own terms. The theory says that competition gives the public what it demands; therefore what the public gets is what it demanded. This form of reasoning is known as *petitio principii*, or begging the question, or assuming what you pretend to prove.

viii

If the invisible hand actually did turn unregulated competition to beneficent ends, the ancient rule of *caveat emptor* should perhaps be resuscitated. Professor Herbert Stein, formerly Chairman of the Council of Economic Advisers, once made a widely retailed *mot* to the effect that people of liberal mind trust anyone over eighteen to vote for President of the United States but don't think the common man or woman capable of buying a bicycle without do-gooding governmental protection.

But a purchase is not a one-way transaction; I don't get a bicycle for nothing. When I buy one from Professor Stein for $199.99, I give him two hundred-dollar bills, and he gives me a penny and the bike. Professor Stein says that I, the *emptor*, should make myself a self-reliant expert on bicycles before I trade in his shop, and that if what he sells me proves dangerous or shoddy, it's my fault, not his.

If so, why shouldn't *caveat emptor* be balanced by *caveat venditor*? If he can (unintentionally or maybe not) sell me a dangerous or shoddy bicycle at my peril, why can't I pay him with counterfeit hundred-dollar bills, at his peril? Or a rubber check? Why shouldn't he be required to make himself a self-reliant expert on these matters, and not go running to the sheriff for help?

Obviously it's no answer to say that counterfeiting is against the law. That law could be repealed, just as the Federal Trade Commission can be hamstrung. Nor is it any answer to say that check bouncing is cheating and so immoral and bad for the soul; the same can be said for selling dangerous bicycles. Nor is it even any answer to say that government regulations impose an intolerable burden of paperwork on the bicycle business. The legal requirement that I have enough money in my account to cover my checks means that I must balance my checkbook, and that's an intolerable burden of paperwork, if you ask me.

Paper money, personal checks, and credit cards have been good for business. They make business easier to transact. Seller and buyer don't need to wear out their teeth biting coins. Within very broad limits, they can trust what is proffered. They can trust, because this is in general a trustworthy society. And it is a trustworthy society in part because the sanctions of the criminal law enforce the trust.

If recipients of rubber checks had to rely on the civil law, they'd be faced with endless delays and absurd costs. They would spend hundreds or thousands of dollars, not to mention hours of court appearances, to get a judgment that they'd still have difficulty collecting. They couldn't afford such costs; so they couldn't afford to accept checks; so they'd have to restrict themselves to much slower and smaller cash-only business. The threat of criminal penalties, enforced by the state, deters check cheats and makes it possible for merchants to trust the rest of us, to the merchants' benefit and ours.

What's sauce for the goose is sauce for the gander. I'd be readier to buy Professor Stein's bicycle if I knew it's safe; and I'd be surer it's safe if I knew the law would crack down on him if it weren't. I can't afford to sue him for damages unless I've been catastrophically hurt, which neither of us wants to happen. Since he really does not intend to cheat me, and I really do not intend to cheat him, we'd both be better off if we knew the law would call those who do cheat to account: we'd both be better able to trust each other.

Perhaps more important: if the law made it possible for me to trust what is offered for sale, I'd no longer have to make dubious reliance on brand names as guarantees of product quality. Then Lewis Mumford's vision of the efficiency of parochial production might become a reality, and so might E. F. Schumacher's vision of the beauty of smallness. Then, too, Ralph Nader would at last be recognized as the champion of the free market.

ix

The great refusal of the stockholders has an apparent parallel in the reluctance of the generality of workers to participate in management. The parallel is only apparent. The stockholders refuse to play a role that is now legally theirs, while the workers are slow to fight for a role that is rightfully theirs.

There are many reasons for this. In the history of American labor relations, workers have been able to improve their lot primarily through tradewide and industrywide unionization. Given what must be reckoned a persistent bias of the courts, the workers have been at the unrestricted mercy of the bosses. Their survival has depended on their solidarity with one another rather than on the prosperity of the firms they work for. Even profit sharing has been looked at askance and usually rejected as a disguised form of the speed-up.

Employee ownership is not without its supporters. In the 1920s Edward A. Filene, searching for a way out of the misery of early twentieth-century industrialism, became a strong advocate of "that democratization upon which social peace and efficiency [a characteristic juxtaposition of the times] must increasingly depend." Accordingly he tried to establish a form of employee ownership in his Boston department store, but was disappointed to discover that most of the employees were not interested or were overawed by a few of their more energetic fellows.

In spite of many such experiences, enthusiasts for employee ownership claim that self-interest will make the employees work harder, and that employee-owned firms will therefore drive conventional corporations out of business. Nothing like this has happened. Self-interest remains undefined; and some employee-owned firms are efficient; some are not. Efficiency is not the issue; justice is.

12

JUSTICE

Why Micro and Macro Don't Mix and How They Can

i

Though the gross national product is a comparatively new idea, and though statistics relating to it have been systematically collected for not much more than fifty years, the term "GNP" has passed into the common vocabulary, where it is frequently invoked as an infallible guide to proper policies. The idea is, however, of severely limited usefulness, and its misuse confuses and misleads public action.

It may be useful to cite a few examples. The 1984 budget for the United States space shuttle and related activities was $6.9 billion. The same amount of money could have paid for roughly 100,000 units of public housing, whose construction, incidentally, would probably have employed more workers than the shuttle. It is a matter of judgment whether more communications satellites are more in the public interest than more housing; but the GNP is of no help in making that judgment, because the two programs have a closely similar effect on the GNP.

Again: The Johns Manville asbestos products swelled the GNP three ways: first, when the products were manufactured and installed; second, when doctors, nurses, hospitals, pharmaceutical manufacturers, lawyers, and insurance adjusters were employed because of the resulting cancers; and third, when workmen were employed in removing the

asbestos installations. Anyone with his eyes solely on the
GNP would be delighted with these results, but they were
catastrophic for many individuals and damaging to the society.

Again: Mark Twain dramatized the irrelevance of the GNP
in his quip about two women who "earned a precarious
living by taking in each other's washing." If a woman renounces home washing and takes a job in a commercial laundry, she thereby increases the GNP. She may also enlarge
her life and increase her contribution to society, but whether
she does so or not will not be discovered by examining the
GNP.

Again: In the 1970s Brazil was widely hailed as a wonderworking economy because of the rapid increase of its GNP.
A decade later, however, it was evident that the country was
essentially bankrupt. Its apparent prosperity, moreover, had
had only adverse effects on the lives of the squatters in the
hillside barrios behind Rio and the sugar workers in the
northeastern provinces. Strict attention to the GNP had misled the world's bankers, who consequently sponsored an
economic as well as a social failure.

Again: If you are a manufacturer of a detergent or of anything else for a broad market, you will find the GNP irrelevant or misleading (as in Brazil). Your proper concern will be
whether there are enough people employed and well enough
paid to buy your product. And if you are a purveyor of diamond bracelets, you will base your output on the number of
millionaires, not on the GNP.

There is nothing in the foregoing that is not well known,
and the examples could be endlessly multiplied. Yet economists and businessmen and public officials maintain their
faith in the GNP. Measures that would protect us from pollution of our environment and damage to our health are routinely opposed because they would, it is said, decrease
production. (Ironically, those who oppose conservation generally call themselves conservatives.) The habit of thought is
pervasive: even so-called liberal economists tend to talk of a
trade-off between a healthful environment and production,

and Third World public officials protest that they cannot "afford" to be concerned with health or safety.

Such trade-offs are only too obvious in one-company towns where the single factory is a gross polluter of air and water. When threatened with laws requiring it to clean up its operations, the company counterthreatens to shut down the plant altogether and thus destroy the town's excuse for existence. Economically, the threat and counterthreat indicate an incompatibility of microeconomics, the economics of the individual or firm, with macroeconomics, the economics of the nation or society.

ii

The division between microeconomics and macroeconomics is well established. It was not always thus. The names of the divisions do not appear in the *Oxford English Dictionary*, published in 1933, or in the second edition of *Webster's New International Dictionary*, whose last issue was copyright in 1953. Now, however, college courses routinely appear under one rubric or the other. What has been put asunder is not easily joined or rejoined.

Indeed, they cannot be joined so long as economic activity is taken to be the maximization of material gain by the individual, the firm, and the nation. That the material interests of these parties are not always identical or even parallel is too obvious to discuss, and consequently is not discussed except in homilies of the sort that everyone recognizes as self-serving. When the boss harangues the workers with the thought that they're all players on the same team, the latter are forewarned of a policy likely to benefit someone else more than it benefits them. When President Eisenhower's Secretary of Defense, Charles E. Wilson, former head of General Motors, piously proclaimed, "What's good for General Motors is good for America," everyone laughed, and the laughter did not need explanation. When the private citizen closets himself with his Form 1040, or the corporation financial officer with Form 1120, neither takes seriously the form's inspiring prefatory message from the Commissioner of Internal Revenue.

It is worth while to stop a minute and note that the foregoing are all typical examples of the fallacy of composition, which is so frequently encountered in economics discussions that it might be called the economics fallacy. The error lies in assuming that what is true of every member of a logical class is true of the class itself, or vice versa, that what is true of a class is true of each of its members. For other examples: since every event has a cause, it is illicitly concluded that all events together—that is, the universe—has a cause. Or in economics, since individuals can become rich by hoarding, the nation will be more prosperous if consumption is discouraged. We shall meet other examples as we explore the relationship of microeconomics to macroeconomics.

The division between the two branches is more than rhetorical. Standard microeconomics holds that the purpose of business enterprise is profit maximization, and it follows as a principle of successful business management that it's sensible to cut your losses. Any fledgling MBA has a quick eye for seeing how any firm's activities can be divided into semi-autonomous "profit centers," and a quick ear for hearing which profit centers are now yielding a desired rate of profit, which ones can be made to do so, and which ones are hopeless. Those in the last category may in fact be profitable; they are just not profitable enough. The minimum acceptable rate of return is the money-market rate. If you can get, say, 10 percent just by lending your money to someone else, why should you go to the bother of running a business that earns less than 10 percent? Or if you do, in the course of your business, borrow money from banks (which is one thing banks are for), and if you pay a rate of a little better than that 10 percent, you're obviously not doing very well with a profit center that doesn't earn more than you pay.

So you are advised to sell the weak profit center if possible, otherwise to liquidate it. You will probably have to take

JUSTICE 145

a loss, but at the current corporation tax rates, more than half of your loss will be paid for by the government via the reduction of your income and hence of your tax bill. The funds thus freed can then be applied to the promising profit centers, or put into the money market, or used to reduce your corporate debt. However you use the funds, the net profit of your company will be improved.

Consider a profit center that is earning 5 percent on invested capital of a million dollars, while the firm's target is 12 percent. Even if the weak profit center—workers, customers, inventory, plant, and all—were abandoned at a total loss, the aftertax result would be that more than a half million dollars would be available for use in the centers that earn 12 percent or more. Twelve percent of a half million dollars is $60,000, while 5 percent of a million is only $50,000.

Such vandalism, which is hailed as "creative destruction," is bad enough in the arena of microeconomics. The workers and the customers are injured, and the inventory and plant—and the work that went into them—wasted in a world of limited resources. The injury and the waste are far greater when macroeconomic problems are approached in the same way. It is said that just as in a firm there are many profit centers so in the nation there are many firms. On this analogy it is widely thought that national policy should be directed toward encouraging strong firms and weeding out weak ones.

Analogy is a seductive form of argument that at best is only suggestive. In the present instances there are two crucial differences between the analogies and the actual world. The first is that what is weeded out by the proposed policies are not tares among the wheat but human beings, people, men and women, fellow citizens. The second is that there is no way, in the actual world in which we live, for new industries, no matter how promising, to replace old industries, no matter how unfruitful, in the twinkling of an eye. The replacing can be done in an equation, on paper, in an instant; but in the real world it takes time. The real world is a world of human beings who exist in time and only in time. The things human beings do or make take time; and the less primitive they are, the more time they take.

Moreover, the write-off against taxes that provides much of the incentive at the micro level does not work at the macro level. A corporation can shift most of its loss onto the other taxpayers, but the national wealth must suffer the entire loss of any destruction.

It would have been absurd to imagine that the Lockheed or Chrysler plants could have been immediately—or ever—converted to producing electronic devices or processing information or whatever industries were expected to take their place. Yet ostensibly responsible citizens did in fact allow themselves to brush aside the fact that tens or hundreds of thousands of fellow citizens would have had their livelihoods destroyed, in most cases forever, and that millions of dollars' worth of plant would have been laid waste as effectively as if it had been bombed. All this destruction would have been in the supposed interest of some new industry that no one could even name. The proposed destruction might have been acceptable—you can't make an omelet without cracking eggs—if anyone had had in mind how and how quickly the displaced people and plants could be restored to usefulness. But no one has the right to bet other people's lives on the hope that something will turn up for them in the long run.

Nor are the macroeconomic effects of creative destruction valid even in the timeless world of classical economics. If the gross national product is the sum of individual productions, then the national total is diminished whenever any of the factors of production is withheld or disbarred. The national product is greater if people are making automobiles inefficiently than if they are doing nothing. It is greater if they are raking leaves than if they are doing nothing. The national product is greater if a plant is producing steel inefficiently than if it is producing nothing. Something is more than nothing; so every additional thing produced increases the gross national product.

Thus profit maximization on the part of a firm may result in diminishing the gross national product. This result is quite independent of the harm done to people. Microeconomics can be—and often is—at war with macroeconomics. This apparent paradox is yet another example of the fallacy of composition. What is good for General Motors is not necessarily good for America, and this is no paradox but a well-understood matter of common observation.

iii

The incompatibility of microeconomics and macroeconomics is particularly stark in discussions of productivity, a problem said in the 1980s to underlie the special problems of the nation's competitiveness in foreign trade and hard-core unemployment at home. The United States was said to be losing out to Japan in a number of industries (especially automobiles) because of falling, or at least not steadily increasing, productivity. And the influx of women, blacks, Hispanics, and young people into the labor force was said, for a variety of invidious reasons, to lower the average competence of the labor force, while the increasing complexity of modern industry made it probable that large numbers of the least competent—perhaps as many as 6 percent of the total labor force—would always be unemployed because unemployable.

At first glance, this account certainly seems plausible; but starting with the very definition of productivity, there are difficulties abounding. There are, to be sure, several ways of defining productivity. They all, however, are of the same general form as the most common one, which takes the GNP for a given period and divides it by the number of hours worked in that period. That the GNP is an unreliable figure we have already said. In the present instance, it must be noticed that the figure of the GNP is stated in terms of money, that the United States GNP is stated in dollars, and the Japanese in yen; and that any com-

parison of the productivity rates of the two countries therefore turns initially on the exchange rates of the currencies. If
the dollar is overvalued, as it was conceded to be in the early
1980s, the United States' productivity rate will be under-
stated in relation to that of other countries, in this case
Japan's.

Putting this initial consideration aside (no doubt refinements can be introduced into the calculations to minimize
the distortion), let us look at the consequences of stating productivity as a function of "hours worked." On this basis, for
example, you have to say that, if a skilled journeyman car-
penter can increase his output 50 percent by taking on an
unskilled apprentice helper, the result is a 25 percent decrease in the productivity of his segment of the economy. It
is on this basis, too, that people say that attention to clean
air and safety decrease productivity and should therefore be
avoided. And it is on this basis that it is solemnly averred
that productivity will be increased by keeping some ten million people unemployed.

A significant fact about any productivity index, whether
of labor or of capital, whether carefully designed or sloppy,
is that it is a ratio, a fraction. There are two ways of increasing the value of any fraction: one can increase the nu-
merator ($\frac{2}{3}$ is greater than $\frac{1}{3}$) or one can decrease the
denominator ($\frac{1}{2}$ is also greater than $\frac{1}{3}$). In microeconomic
terms, one can increase a firm's profitability either by increasing sales or by decreasing expenses. In times of recession or depression, surviving firms will generally choose the
latter option and will pay particular attention to holding
down wage levels and especially to pruning the labor force
wherever possible.

As President Coolidge pontificated, "When many people
are out of work, unemployment results," and this truism
points to another conflict between microeconomics and macroeconomics. For unemployment caused in the way we have
described is plainly in the interest of the firm and equally
plainly contrary to the interest of the nation, and the attempt
to bring them together at this point is another example of

the fallacy of composition. If maximization of material gain is the goal, it will always be in the interest of the nation to increase output, while it is often in the interest of the firm to decrease employment and output.

Most discussion of productivity is confused on this point, which may be put in another way: A proper concern of a firm's management is the productivity of its work force, which may be properly, though roughly, stated as the firm's output divided by "hours worked." But the proper concern of a national administration is with national productivity, which could be reasonably stated as GNP divided, not by the hours worked, but by the total work force—full time, part time, unemployed, and unemployable—or by the national population. After all, the N in GNP stands for "National"; it includes us all. If the calculation is not based on something like the GNP per person, we may drift, as many of us do drift, into thinking that national productivity is increased by decreasing the denominator, that is, by policies that tolerate, and even create, large numbers of unemployed.

In short, the distinction between microeconomics and macroeconomics is by no means a sterile theoretical question, but one that has profound consequences in the lives we live.

iv

It is obvious that whatever I do will have some effect on the firm for which I work, that whatever the firm does will have some effect on the gross national product, that whatever the nation does will have some effect on me and my firm. It is equally obvious that these effects are not all always in the same direction or of comparable strength.

The direction and importance of the effects depend on the purpose pursued. If health is my concern, healthy working conditions and a healthy general environment are in my interest. And in the other direction, if the nation is concerned for the health of the population as a whole, it will be in its interest to control the pollution emitted by factories and to try to eliminate communicable diseases. There is no conflict among these purposes; they all work together. Purposes with a similar unity of effect would include education, efficient communications, safety from violence, among many others. Often there are limited conflicts that can be compromised; thus, an improved highway may require taking a person's home by eminent domain, and the compensation offered by the state in a given instance may not be reasonable, but there is no difficulty with the principle involved.

With the maximization of material gain, as we have seen, the situation is quite different. Person, firm, and nation may be, and often are, at cross purposes. Nevertheless, in modern times the maximization of material gain has been thought the proper objective of economic activity. In pursuit of that objective, conservatives have emphasized the creative power of individual energy, and liberals have emphasized the organizing power of the state.

As a practical matter, the conservative-liberal confrontation was considerably papered over during the past hundred years, and especially during the quarter century following World War II. An extraordinary increase in gross productivity lent plausibility to the metaphor President John F. Kennedy borrowed from Prime Minister Winston Churchill: "A rising tide raises all ships." Although the relative shares of the national product scarcely changed, the absolute increase in the total—from $209.8 billion in 1946 to $1,077.6 billion in 1971 (even in so-called constant dollars the increase was 135 percent)—allowed almost everyone to benefit dramatically. The subsequent years, however, saw the ships rising unequally, with many sinking.

That some of the exaggerated inequality was deliberately brought about only confirms the judgment that, in terms of material gain, microeconomics and macroeconomics are not systematically connected. It must be emphasized that a statistical covariance does not demonstrate a systematic connection, especially if the covariance fluctuates, as this one in fact does. There was no reason for the record-breaking 735,000 individuals and firms that in 1983 were petitioners in bankruptcy to be cheered by the so-called recovery of that year. There was no reason for the 320,000 new millionaires of the years 1976 through 1980 to be upset by the stagflation of that period.

There is no reason for starving people to be cheered by a rising GNP. For the starving people to be reconciled to their fate, they would have to be shown not only that the national prosperity was enhanced by their starvation, but also that their sacrifice was the salvation of their fellow citizens and of the nation that nurtured them. Such a showing can be made to a soldier in time of war. But no one pretends that such a showing can be made in economics at any time.

v

It should not surprise us to have to conclude that if maximization of material gain is the objective of economic activity, no unification of microeconomics and macroeconomics is possible. Maximization of gain is an undefinable and meaningless concept.

But, if economics is a division of ethics and justice is its goal, the two subdisciplines come together readily enough. Indeed, they must come together, because they cannot then maintain themselves separately. Ethics is neither an exclusively private affair nor an exclusively social affair; it involves both individual and society because they define each other. Not only do individual and society define each other, but the mutual definitions are framed in ethical terms. The state requires certain actions and forbids many actions, all in the interest of maintaining just and civil relations among its citizens. The citizens demand that the state do this.

What just and civil relations may be is a historical question. The standards were developed in time and exist in time. More important, they are historical because the future is uncertain and unknowable. The "separate but equal" doctrine of *Plessy* v. *Ferguson* seemed wise and just to most people in 1896; it turned out to have unjust consequences and was overturned in *Brown* v. *Board of Education* in 1954. Every individual action and every social institution is inexorably subject to similar limitation.

13

INFLATION

The Disease and a Cure

i

If there is a dead hand lying upon contemporary economic thought, it is the invisible hand discovered by Adam Smith. Two hundred years ago, this was, as we saw in the first chapter, a liberating hand, which participated in freeing men from arbitrary rulers. But it did so at the ultimate cost of conceiving of men and women as servomechanisms. There has been the further cost of diverting public policy away from direct action on perceived ills. This diversion has been occasioned partly by the classical economic view that the economy automatically tends toward an optimum equilibrium, partly by the classical scientific recognition that nature to be controlled must be obeyed, and partly by the classical legal view that the law should forbid but seldom direct.

But if it is not in our stars that we are underlings; if we are the captains of our souls; if, as we have said more prosaically, we are autonomous, then the ban on direct action loses its force. In any case, its force is only illusory, for any policy, whether direct or indirect, is a control, an interference. It is not natural but human. It has consequences for which human beings are responsible. And the consequences of inaction or of indirect action are no different in kind or degree from those of direct action. The consequences of failing to act directly are often appalling.

153

An ill that everyone perceives as such is unemployment. Some emphasize the hurt to society when people, whether willfully or not, live without working. Others emphasize the hurt to individuals who are not permitted to make a contribution to, or to enjoy the privileges of, society. Both hurts are severe and unquestioned. Yet they are permitted to exist, to continue, to grow. Sometimes, as in the United States in the early 1980s, they are deliberately exacerbated.

A people-oriented political economy would take direct action on this problem; a pseudo-science approaches the problem indirectly. In the direct approach, the government creates the needed jobs, paying a decent wage even when the work is indecent. The naïve reaction to such a program is a cry of horror at the cost and the prospect of waste. A more sophisticated reaction resorts to some variation of the Phillips Curve linking full employment to inflation. A cynical reaction accepts Marx's charge that capitalism needs the industrial reserve army of the unemployed to keep the workers in check.

The sad fact is that only the last of these reactions has any empirical evidence to support it. Where direct action has been tentatively tried, as in the early New Deal, the cost of the program was not substantially greater than the cost of inaction. The budget deficit in 1932, the last Hoover year, was $2.7 billion, while in 1940, the last pre-war year, it was $3.1 billion. In the meantime, thousands of schools, libraries, hospitals, post offices, dams, and other public buildings were built. Electricity was brought to the farms. A start was made on public housing. Thousands of miles of highways were constructed. Thousands of square miles of public lands were improved by the CCC. Hundreds of pictures were painted; scores of plays were produced; uncounted amounts of literary and historical material were collected, preserved, and made available for study; fifty or more guidebooks were published, many of which have not been superseded a half century later. And millions of men and women were enabled to make a contribution to society. The extent of these contributions is obscured by the statistical quirk whereby those who worked for the WPA, CCC, NYA, and the rest of the so-called alphabet soup are evidently counted as unemployed.

Of course there was waste. There is waste in private industry, waste in private homes; life is wasteful. It is safe to say that the Pentagon now wastes more in a month than Dr. New Deal did in the entire eight years before being replaced by Dr. Win-the-War. But that is not the point. Nor is it relevant that most of the nongovernment art of the period, like most of the WPA art, no longer satisfies our esthetic taste. The point is that millions of people were enabled to preserve their self-respect.

There is also an ordinary economic side to all this. While any form of relief increases consumption and so stimulates production (priming the pump, as FDR said), the dole forgoes the initial stimulus and the ultimate value, whatever it may be, of the public works themselves. As Keynes remarked, "Pyramid-building, earthquakes, even wars may serve to increase wealth, if the education of our statesmen on the principles of classical economics stand in the way of anything better. . . . It would, indeed, be more sensible to build homes and the like."

ii

It is now generally agreed that, given a modicum of compassion, some form of relief will be forever necessary. The poor we have always with us. People today argue whether full employment is reached with 6 percent or more unemployed. Seldom is the figure any longer set as low as 4 percent (which is what economists used to have in mind), though the actual figure was lower than that in eight of the ten years immediately following World War II, and again in the four years from 1966 through 1969. The fact that many (not all) of those years were years of Korea and Vietnam doesn't signify. Pyramid building—or home building—would have done just as well.

Classical economics claimed that a truly free economy would always tend toward true full employment. A slump would of course throw people out of work; but they would therefore lower their wage demands until it became profitable for entrepreneurs to reemploy them, whereupon a prosperous equilibrium would be reestablished. According to this line of reasoning, still favored by ultra-conservatives, minimum-wage and minimum-hour laws, union contracts, and even home relief, all interfere with the natural equilibrium and so prolong the suffering they're supposed to alleviate. One trouble with this theory is that there will always be a minimum wage after all, no matter how willing the unemployed are to cooperate in achieving equilibrium. That irreducible minimum wage is subsistence; if workers can't survive, they can't work. Of course, they could probably make do with a lot less than they think they can. But there is a minimum nevertheless.

A more fundamental—one might say more businesslike—objection to the classical theory was sketched by Keynes and developed more fully by Professor Paul Davidson in his book *Money and the Real World*. In the real world, where business is actually done, time is always a factor. Everything takes time, and so everything requires planning for the future. Retail stores buy ahead for delivery in a few days, weeks, or months. Manufacturers work even farther ahead in buying raw materials and much farther ahead in ordering new machinery. All of this ordering takes the form of contracts with prices stated. Prices are stated in terms of money.

This is the way business is actually done and the way it is inevitably done, because the future is systematically unknown. However rational one may be in one's expectations, one would be foolhardy to order machinery without knowing its price, especially since one usually has the option of buying secondhand machinery or a whole plant at some known current price. On the other side, one would be foolhardy to manufacture specialized and expensive machinery without an order in hand. To get the order, the machinery manufacturer must set the price; and to set the price, he must be confident that he will have a competent work force at settled wages. And this will also be true of all the subcontractors on whom he must rely. It is therefore not at all in the interest of business that wage scales should fluctuate widely in search of a supposed equilibrium.

Wages will consequently be the subject of contract negotiations and will not always be left to the vagaries of the hypothetical market. The market being bypassed in this manner, the doctrinaire objections to government interference in that market disappear, and it becomes possible to consider the government's being at all times the employer of last resort, offering decent wages, regardless of the presumed necessity of the work done, though it would certainly be good public policy to try to arrange work as useful as possible. Given the present deterioration in public facilities, there is plenty to be done. By way of example, the federal government might pay a city to keep its libraries and museums open longer hours, to collect its garbage more frequently, to expand its police and fire protection, to run cleaner buses and subways on denser schedules—all of which used to be done in less boastfully affluent times. City blocks that now stand vacant could be turned into temporary (or permanent) playgrounds, in some of which it would be possible to have the equivalent of the old swimming hole. The reason why such things are not done now is that work relief, when it is available, is paid at (or below) the minimum wage (in New York, homeless men were recently paid 85 cents an hour). After all, anyone who seeks relief is a beggar, and beggars can't be choosers. The objection to having relief workers do the jobs indicated comes not from those on relief but very properly from those presently employed, who understandably fear political pressure to reduce their pay to the relief level. This fear would disappear if relief work were paid regular wages rather than minimum wages, and relief workers could then be given useful rather than "noncompetitive" work.

No doubt a policy like the foregoing would cost money.

Yet the armed services and the space program cost money, too, and it is reasonably argued that these programs make jobs and so contribute to general prosperity. They are like the pyramids in this. Decently paid relief work would make at least as great a contribution to general prosperity and in addition would contribute to the common wealth.

Indirect tinkering with the economy to stimulate saving or investment acknowledges that it would still leave one in sixteen, or maybe more, not only unemployed but without hope of employment. This is not good enough for a nation that calls itself civilized.

iii

A side effect widely expected to follow upon full employment, especially including government-sustained full employment, is inflation. "Side effect" is of course a medical metaphor; and it may be remarked by the way that economists seem addicted (another medical metaphor) to such usages. Still another such metaphor likens the boom phase of the business cycle to a debauch that poisons the body politic and must be cured by massive purgation. There are those who say that the purge will follow anyhow, and that nature should be allowed to run its course. Others prescribe an economic *nux vomica* or, more vividly, a bloodletting, in order to hasten the process. It is necessary, they say, to induce present illness in the interest of future health.

The Hippocratic Oath includes the words "The regime I adopt shall be for the benefit of my patients . . . and not for their hurt." Those responsible for economic policy—and that includes economists, politicians, and businessmen—should take such an oath, for heartless economic policy has caused more suffering in the world even than heartless medicine.

Since medical metaphors are widely relied on as telling arguments, it is perhaps worth remarking that medicine has long recognized that bloodletting and purges weaken a patient to no avail and thus delay or prevent rather than hasten the recovery. More to the point, one might heed the solid common sense of Keynes, who said, "The right remedy for the trade cycle is not to be found in abolishing booms and thus keeping us permanently in a semi-slump; but in abolishing slumps and thus keeping us permanently in a quasi-boom."

Inflation is the aspect of booms that has attracted the most attention for almost half a century. This long preoccupation with inflation is evidence of a profound confusion of American will—indeed, the confusion has been practically worldwide. Inflation is not an evil in itself; some evils may follow in its train, but no particular evil necessarily does. Evils, moreover, are always specific, not general, and are therefore open to specific treatment, while the chosen attacks on inflation have systematically damaged all sectors of the economy, with the possible exception of banking.

In the public discussions of inflation, the evil that has had the most attention is the erosion of the standard of living of retired people and others said to be living on a fixed income. Here is a specific evil that can be assessed and a cure proposed. In fact, this evil was assessed; cures were proposed; and the cures, the first of which has been in effect since 1966, have been remarkably successful. In 1966 Medicare began to protect the aged from one of the most crushing burdens of old age and at the same time to provide millions with health care that otherwise would have been denied them; in 1972 and 1973, automatic cost-of-living increases were legislated for Social Security payments. Since these increases were tied to the Consumer Price Index, and since the CPI was badly skewed because of the excessive weight it gave to the mortgage rate, and since the elderly are in general not borrowers anyhow, there is no doubt that many retired persons were better off in 1980 than they had been ten or more years previously. To be sure, a great hue and cry, led by a committee of investment bankers, persuaded the nation that the elderly had it too good, and managed to raise Social Security taxes and lower benefits. That is not the point. The point is that the urgency of doing something about inflation was said to turn on damage done to the elderly. Granting the damage, something was done about it. If what was done was considered too much (or too little), that only reinforces the argument that specific cures *can* be devised for specific ailments. There was no need to adopt monetary policies that ravaged the economy of the nation and of the world in order to address the problems of a small (though growing) segment of the population.

The recent attacks on Social Security have traded on the confusion that has existed since the program's New Deal beginnings. From the start, it has been partly an insurance (or endowment) program, and partly a welfare program. Social Security taxes are a form of forced premium payments; yet the benefits are not strictly proportional to the premiums. The attacks on the program have concentrated on its insurance aspect, making much of the fact that the increased benefits of the past two decades have, or may soon have, depleted the fund from which they are drawn. The "bankruptcy" of the program is foretold, especially in view of the aging of the population. To avoid this alleged bankruptcy, taxes have been raised and benefits reduced.

This is all very well, but it is flatly subversive of any attempt to solve the problems of those living on a fixed income in a time of even very low inflation. With an annual inflation rate of only 3 percent (which is sometimes said to be the long-term rate), average prices will rise roughly 40 percent over a ten-year period. Such an increase can be disastrous for people living on a fixed income. If, at the same time, benefits are reduced, the disaster is obviously compounded.

Thus policies—of whatever sort—that bring inflation down to its long-term rate may mitigate but cannot solve the problems of people living on fixed incomes. If solving those problems is a sincere objective of policy, they must be addressed directly, as they were in 1966, 1972, and 1973. Our experience since those years shows that such direct action, emphasizing the welfare aspect of Social Security, can be successful.

Many of course have scruples against promoting the general welfare and so want to emphasize the insurance aspect of Social Security. They cannot then honorably use the plight of the elderly as their reason for supporting draconian measures against inflation, because the draconian measures hurt the elderly along with everyone else. They may have other reasons for supporting draconian measures, but the plight of the elderly cannot reasonably be one of them.

To be sure, the elderly are not the only people living on fixed incomes. There are the widows and orphans, over whom many tears were shed in the opposition to New Deal controls on the stock exchanges, the banks, and the utility holding companies. Crocodile tears aside, this problem is admittedly wider than that of Ferdinand Lundberg's sixty American families of great wealth. Addressing the wider problem, it might be urged that the welfare aspect of Social Security be broadened to cover such of these citizens as are not now covered. Beyond this, it must be acknowledged that people who live on fixed incomes—whether the result of savings or of inheritance—have no greater claim to immunity to the vicissitudes of life than do those who work for a living. As it has actually happened, the programs that have been undertaken in the announced interest of controlling inflation have in fact caused—and were intended to cause—widespread unemployment. At the same time, the soaring interest rate—which was deliberately encouraged to soar—has offered opportunities for aggrandizement (not always taken, to be sure) to those with funds laid by. In short, the policies actually adopted have favored unearned income over earned income; that is, those whom Keynes, following R. H. Tawney, called functionless investors, over those who do the current work of the world.

iv

One of the signs of the confusion about inflation is the tendency to see it as a simple phenomenon with a simple explanation. In the classical view, it is primarily a monetary question, as David Hume argued in 1752 in one of the first expositions of the quantity theory of money. If it were decreed that every dollar we have today could be redeemed tomorrow for two dollars, we could expect that soon thereafter all prices would have doubled. A slight modification of this model gives us the familiar "too much money chasing too few goods." When the wheat crop—or the distribution thereof—failed in pre-Revolutionary France, the demand for bread bid the price of wheat up catastrophically. (But the price of many other commodities fell as people desperately tried to raise money to pay for bread.)

The inflation that has beset the world in the second half of the twentieth century followed none of these scenarios. There has been no shortage of things to buy. Temporary or local shortages—most notably of petroleum—did certainly exist, but they did not last long, and in general store shelves have been heavily laden with groceries and with dry goods. Prices were nevertheless high, too high for most people, and so trade was slow and became slower. If people don't have enough money to buy what is offered for sale, it is silly to claim that too much money is chasing too few goods.

Since the modern inflation unquestionably exists, and since the classical explanation of prices being pulled up by demand does not hold, it seems sensible to look in the direction of cost-push inflation. The cost that has attracted the most attention is the cost of labor. It is, after all, the most important single cost, running at about 80 percent of the net national income, or about 65 percent of GNP.

A lot of work has been done on a theory that says that money wages can go up without affecting money prices so long as the real productivity of labor goes up at the same rate. If real productivity doesn't go up that fast—or even falls—prices have to go up to compensate. This seems straightforward enough. But there are problems, the most difficult of which is the fact that the real product, as we have said, is not a determinable quantity, even in a particular industry such as boilermaking. If one attempts to add apples and pears to boilers, one is in even worse case, and so real productivity is not a determinable quantity.

To be sure, the quantity seems to have been determined, because there are tables purporting to show its variation over the years. But what we have in these tables are the results of elaborate estimates, or guesses, or of calculations that note the rise of money wages and of prices and that reason therefrom that productivity has fallen. In the latter case, productivity is not the result of what workers do (which is what it appears to be) but the solution of an equation. Harder or more devoted work won't necessarily improve it, and inflation wouldn't necessarily be cured if it could be improved. Thus various proposals to control inflation by controlling wages suffer from the usual ills of the indirect approach.

The mark of inflation is rising prices, not rising wages. We can have—indeed, do actually have—continuing inflation far above the long-term rate even though wage scales are falling and have been falling for several years. It may be true, as economists from Keynes to Weintraub have noticed, that there is a tendency for prices and wages to spiral up together. Professor Weintraub's studies convinced him that prices are set at a relatively constant markup over unit wage costs, but the perceived constancy can only be fortuitous. It is not engraved in granite that labor's share of the national income should be 80 percent, rather than more, or less.

If inflation is a problem, the place to put in the chisel is at the price level. If you control prices, you *ipso facto* control inflation, because price rises are what inflation is. Controlling prices might also force each corporation and very likely the economy as a whole to look carefully at the wage markup and at other ratios that rule or seem to rule income distribution. The result might be a decline in dividends and a shakedown of executive salaries and perquisites. If so, that would doubtless be all to the good; but if inflation is the issue, prices (or selected prices) should be controlled no matter what the effect on income distribution. Income distribution is a separate problem and should, in its turn, be treated directly. It might develop, as Galbraith believes on the basis of his experience with OPA during the war, that you would have to control wages as well as prices, but the control of prices is the object in the control of inflation.

v

Income distribution is undoubtedly a more important problem than inflation, and the present badly skewed distribution is certainly not without its effect on inflation. When a corporation CEO arranges a multi-million-dollar salary for himself, he is shamed into doing very well for his immediate subordinates, who must do well for theirs, and so on down the line; and these inflated salaries don't pass unnoticed during union wage negotiations. Thus the entire payroll is inflated, and cost-push inflation is given another boost upward.

However all that may be, there are other grounds for insisting that someday a start should be made on narrowing the gap between the rich and the poor. It is often said that the gap is not really significant because taking from the rich and giving to the poor would not give the poor a great deal more than they have now (while the incentive of the rich would be sapped). This may once have been true, but it is far from the truth today. In 1981 the total of personal incomes in the United States was $2,435 billion. If this sum has been equally divided among the 229,849,000 people then living in the country, a family of four would have had an income of $42,375. In the same year, the official poverty level for a family of four (families of four are always talked about, though they are no longer the norm) was $9,287, and there were 31,800,000 people living *below* that level. Also in the same year, the average production-line worker, working full time (which comparatively few did), earned $13,270; and there was much talk in high places to the effect that such people were overpaid.

Hardly anyone proposes absolute equality of income, but it is not difficult to suggest reasonable guidelines. We can say, first, that everyone's self-respect depends on his or her making a contribution (not necessarily economic) to society, and that society should make such contributions possible. We can say, next, that everyone is entitled to compensation in rough proportion to his or her contribution. We add, however, that with a tiny handful of possible exceptions no one is indispensable, and so no one (including the indispensable persons) is entitled to outrageous compensation, nor should anyone be denied a decent minimum.

Today the chasm is so great that even tax rates approaching those of World War II could not throw much of a bridge across it. This does not mean that such rates (of course with different brackets to reflect the intervening inflation) should not be enacted; it merely means something more will be necessary, possibly setting, as President Roosevelt suggested during the war, an absolute upper limit to income. Because disparities of wealth are even greater than those of income, estate taxes approaching confiscation are not unthinkable and would cause little harm to anyone who has actually earned his wealth. Naturally, the widows and orphans of the wealthy would have to be taken care of, very likely better than the widows and orphans of ordinary citizens. No widow or orphan can believe herself or himself worthy of the wealth of the Rockefellers or in need of such wealth. And if an inability to bequeath such wealth had inhibited the original John D. from working as hard as he did in the ways that he did, no reflective citizen can believe that the economy, the nation, or the world would have been the worse for it. Even the mighty achievements of Rockefeller University, indirectly financed as they were by tax dollars, could have been directly financed with the same dollars, as the National Institutes of Health are today.

What can be said of the Rockefellers' lack of personal importance can hardly be denied of the Hunts and others one might name.

Because of their size and immortality, corporations have more power over our freedom than do individuals. It must therefore be said that the United States has pursued unwise policies in pressing favors on corporations. Their share of federal taxes has declined from 27.6 percent in the 1950s to

5.9 percent in 1983. As states and municipalities have competed in making themselves attractive to business, they, too, have expanded the services they offer corporations and have reduced the share they ask corporations to pay. On all levels, the result has been increased taxation of the middle classes and even of the poor, and this shift in the tax burden has prompted blind tax revolts that, like the federal tax law of 1981 and Proposition 13 in California, have only exacerbated the problem. If the American commonweal is in danger, it is because of our failure to tax corporations progressively and to set appropriate limits to their powers. More than one society has been destroyed at the height of its glory by those who were its principal beneficiaries.

vi

An incidental reason for a more egalitarian distribution of income is that it stimulates production, the expectation being that the poor spend practically all of any additional income they get, while the rich are already spending all that they can. The increased expenditures lead merchants to expand and then to replenish their inventories, whereupon manufacturers have to expand, and so on. The various expansions require additional employment, presumably at higher wages, thus making still more money available for consumption. And so on again. This (very roughly) is Kahn's idea of the multiplier, which holds that production will increase exponentially under the stimulus of increased consumption.

The superficially similar, though diametrically opposite, view holds that production creates its own demand. This is Say's Law, the creation of Jean Baptiste Say, a French contemporary of Adam Smith's. According to Say, when entrepreneurs build a factory and install machinery in it and start manufacturing things, they must pay the workers who do the building and installing and manufacturing, whereupon the workers buy other things from other producers, and so on. In the end, someone will have enough money to buy whatever it was the entrepreneurs produced, and production will have created its own demand.

This scenario is superficially like that of Kahn's multiplier. Say, however, makes three basic assumptions that do not fit the real world. These are (1) goods are really exchanged for goods; money is only a screen for what really happens; (2) any good can be substituted for any other, so that it doesn't much matter what is produced; and (3) the whole operation is in effect accomplished instantaneously, so that there is no problem with synchronization of the various steps. "Thus," concludes Say, in words that could have come from a speech before the National Association of Manufacturers, "it is the aim of good government to stimulate production, of bad government to encourage consumption."

And, in general, conservative businessmen confess belief in Say's notions, though their actions belie their words. They are true Keynesians in spite of themselves, for no one produces except what he expects to sell. If there are already unsalable inventories of a certain product and idle factories capable of making more of it, only a fool would invest in another such factory. Modern corporations may be able, as Galbraith says, to control the market for their products, but they cannot create a market where no purchasing power exists. Thus, regardless of beliefs fervently expounded, no one acts on the basis of Say's Law. Say himself acknowledged that "there is nothing to be got by dealing with people who have nothing to pay." Even so, Say held that a "universal glut"—that is, a depression—was impossible; there is some evidence to the contrary.

14

PROTECTION

How the Multinationals Are Different

i

Ever since Adam Smith, economists have been practically unanimous in support of free trade. Writing in the year of American Independence, Smith declared that "Great Britain derives nothing but loss from the dominion which she assumes over her colonies." The loss came not only from the cost of defending and administering the colonies but also from the higher prices that British exporters could charge because of their monopoly. Higher prices in the colonies induced higher prices at home; so all non-exporters suffered.

For Smith, foreign trade was of minor importance, anyhow. It served two main purposes: it enabled countries to exchange surpluses, and it facilitated the division of labor by expanding the market. In furtherance of these ends he opposed the monopolies and restraints on, or inducements to, trade that were root and branch of the mercantile system. He argued that the Corn Laws, in raising the price of bread, raised the price of almost all domestic manufactures because the minimum wage had to cover the cost of survival; consequently not even landlords were gainers (except to the extent that they used imported goods) because of the increase in price of the things they had to buy.

Over the past two hundred years the domestic market in any one of a score of countries has become larger than the

168

largest world market Smith could have imagined, and the division of labor has gone far beyond the eighteen operations in the manufacture of pins that he immortalized. More important, the merchant adventurers of his day have been supplanted by today's multinational corporations. Nevertheless, his arguments for free trade still circulate and in the United States have inspired a tradition running from John Hay's Open Door in China, through Cordell Hull's Reciprocal Trade Treaties, to the postwar General Agreement on Tariffs and Trade.

ii

David Ricardo was perhaps of even greater importance than Adam Smith to the cause of free trade. In 1817 he published *The Principles of Political Economy and Taxation*, one of the most influential books in the history of the subject. In it he advanced his famous Law of Comparative Advantage, which purports to demonstrate that international trade is mutually profitable even when one country is absolutely more productive in terms of every commodity traded.

On the face of it, this proposition seems implausible, but Ricardo explained it this way: Suppose that a certain amount of wine exchanges for a certain amount of cloth. Suppose that in England it would take a year's labor of 100 men to make the cloth, and of 120 men to make the wine, while in Portugal the man-years required are 90 and 80 respectively. In these circumstances, it would be to Portugal's advantage to make only wine and England's to make only cloth, with the countries then exchanging the surpluses. Portugal would multiply its wine output 2.125 times ([90 + 80] ÷ 80), and England its cloth production 2.2 times, and since the cloth and the wine are equal in value, both countries would come out ahead.

Ricardo was quick to concede that his law applied only to international trade. "Such an exchange," he observed, "could not take place between the individuals of the same country.

The labour of 100 Englishmen cannot be given for that of 80 Englishmen, but the produce of the labour of 100 Englishmen may be given for the produce of the labour of 80 Portuguese, 60 Russians, or 120 East Indians. The difference in this respect, between a single country and many, is easily accounted for, by considering the difficulty with which capital moves from one country to another, to seek a more profitable employment, and the activity with which it invariably passes from one province to another in the same country."

Ricardo went on to declare that "feelings, which I should be sorry to see weakened, induce most men to be satisfied with a low rate of profits in their own country, rather than seek a more advantageous employment for their wealth in foreign countries."

What Ricardo could not foresee, and what his modern followers have overlooked, is that the new multinational corporations fail to share the feelings of patriotism or indeed of prudence that he ascribed (somewhat naïvely even in the nineteenth century) to the capitalists of his time. Today capital flits freely from here to there, moving as indifferently from the United States to Singapore as it did in Ricardo's day from London to Yorkshire.

This is not the only weakness of the law as a guide to modern policy. More important is the fact that, although the law begins by considering historical data (the prices of the wine and the cloth and the numbers of workers engaged in producing them), it ends by assuming that the industrial changes it recommends can be accomplished in an instant and without other consequence—in a word, ahistorically. The British vintners are immediately to become weavers, and the Portuguese weavers vintners. The British wine presses are immediately changed into looms, and the Portuguese looms into wine presses. Such transformation was perhaps almost imaginable in the first quarter of the nineteenth century. Even then, if the transformations were not accomplished immediately, in a trice, both parties would have unemployed workers and unutilized factories, as well as shortages of both wine and cloth. The resulting suffering and

waste would more than offset the promised 6 or 10 percent
increase in output, which could easily be accomplished in
many less traumatic ways.

Like so much of classical economics, the Law of Comparative Advantage is suited to a world without time, where
everything happens all at once, or not at all.

iii

Today, as in the eighteenth and nineteenth centuries, the
more-developed countries need the less-developed countries
as sources of raw materials, some of which are not available
elsewhere. The multinational corporations also use the
LDCs, or some of them, as sources of cheap labor and cheap
working conditions. The banks of the First World find the
feeble nations of the Third World eager borrowers of money
at high interest rates. What was, before independence, imperialism is now neo-imperialism.

There has long been a lively debate about whether gunboat imperialism was good for the mother countries. Adam
Smith, as we have seen, thought not. Bismarck concurred.
"All the advantages claimed for the mother country," he
said, "are for the most part illusions." People as various as
Cecil Rhodes and Hjalmar Schacht were among those who
disagreed.

The Marxian position, scarcely developed by Marx and
Engels, was given shape by J. A. Hobson, by Lenin, by
Rudolf Hilferding, by Rosa Luxemburg, and finally by Stalin. In the end the emphasis was on the imperialist wars that
were expected to be the last stage of capitalism; but initially
and fundamentally it was argued that mature capitalism
needed overseas outlets for investments discouraged at
home by the alleged law of diminishing returns, and overseas markets for goods that couldn't be sold at home because
labor wasn't paid enough.

All sides acknowledged that the colonies were more or less
mistreated, perhaps in the course of the white man's civiliz-

ing mission, perhaps because of white men's inherent viciousness. Cultivated Brahmans were insulted by half-educated British majors. Belgium kept the subject peoples of the Congo in ignorance. And so on. All this was bad, but it should have ended—and largely did end—with the political liberation of the colonies. Yet neo-imperialism took the place of imperialism.

It is possible now to see that the vice of gunboat imperialism was not so much the social and political domination as the economic extraction. It was always easy to see that the resources of the colonies were extracted. What was extracted was paid for at going world prices, which somehow were almost always low. Farmers everywhere are seldom able to demand good prices because they are too dispersed for easy organization, their industry is relatively inexpensive to enter, and their products have many substitutes and are perishable and at the mercy of the weather. What is true of farming is also largely true of mining. The farming and mining industries struggle under these difficulties even in the United States, but here they have been able to organize political power to obtain some relief. Nothing like this has proved possible internationally, with the exceptions of OPEC and the diamond cartel.

What is new about neo-imperialism is the influx of the multinational corporations, especially in the Orient. There have of course been international business organizations for hundreds of years. The old-line companies were in agriculture, like the United Fruit Company, or mining, like Cerro Chemicals. The new multinationals are engaged in manufacturing, and they are first and foremost international marketing organizations having close connections with retail chains and ready access to big finance. It is no secret why the multinationals have moved into the Third World. They are seldom interested in natural resources (they may buy Philippine mahogany, but they ship it to Korea to be turned into plywood for sale in the United States). They certainly are not in search of capital or of technology. As everyone knows, the factor of production that attracts them is labor—

labor that is cheap, unorganized, and undemanding, willing to work long hours for low wages in substandard conditions. The vaunted skill of Chinese surgeons in re-attaching severed fingers and even arms comes from having had plenty of practice.

Thus the distinguishing mark of neo-imperialism is the extraction of labor power. This comes about because the things the multinationals manufacture in the Third World are sold in the First World. The plastic-frame irons General Electric manufactures in Singapore are sold in American discount houses. The steel produced by new Brazilian mills is bought in markets formerly served by Pittsburgh. The textbooks printed in Hong Kong are studied in British classrooms. The California sports shirts run up in Korea are sold in—California. In short, the Marxian theory of imperialism doesn't fit what is going on now. The multinationals are not looking for markets in the Third World; they are looking for labor. The markets—most of the time—are still in the First World.

As a result of all this activity, the Third World has things to export, though it seems never enough. The reason why there is never enough is that the exports to the First World are paid for with imports from the First World. It is at this point that the extraction of labor shows itself, for many times as much labor goes into the exports as into the imports.

The wage differential of course varies from country to country and from industry to industry, but a very rough idea of comparative wage rates can be gathered from the figures the World Bank publishes on GNP per capita. In 1981, for a few examples, the figures were $300 in the People's Republic of China, $790 in the Philippines, $1700 in the Republic of Korea, $2200 in Brazil, and $5240 in Singapore. In the United States the figure was $12,820 (Denmark, West Germany, Norway, Sweden, and Switzerland were all from 2.3 percent to 36.0 percent higher). On the basis of these figures we'll not be overstating the case if we say that a dollar commands five times as much labor in the Third World as it does in the First World. This means that, when the two worlds exchange goods, the Third World is the net loser of four-fifths of the labor involved. This four-fifths is extracted and gone forever. Consequently it is not surprising that the gap between the two worlds is steadily widening.

It is this extraction of labor power that is the vice of neo-imperialism. It is very likely true that the multinationals, or some of them, are not above diddling their books so that they can declare their profits where taxes are lowest. It is certainly true that the international banks, or some of them, are capable of persuading—even bribing—naïve or corrupt Third World officials to borrow money at ultra-usurious rates to build power lines to nowhere and skyscrapers among mud huts. It is also true that the International Monetary Fund will then counsel austerity (meaning a widening of the wage differential) for the hapless citizens of the countries accepting the loans. There is little in these activities of which the participants can be proud, but their effects are small in comparison with the effect of the extraction of labor power.

iv

Those advocating the industrialization of the Third World have had before them a working model of how it can be done. The development of the fledgling United States was financed by loans from England and, to a lesser extent, from the Continent. For a century and a quarter, until World War I, the United States was a debtor nation. American canals and railroads, American steel mills and thread factories, American shipyards and coal mines, all relied on foreign capital. Sometimes the foreigners were swindled, as in the Crédit Mobilier, but usually they got their money back with interest. The United States was a good investment for foreigners, and the investments were good for the United States.

But the nineteenth-century United States model does not fit today's Third World. The difference is simple. The industry financed by today's multinationals manufactures goods for export. In contrast, the infrastructure built in the United

States with foreign capital was necessarily used in the United States; it could not be exported. Moreover, almost all the goods produced in foreign-financed factories were sold and used in the United States. Britain imported food and raw materials from America, but very little in the way of manufactures.

Ironically, America after the Civil War is almost a copybook example of the Marxian theory of imperialism. Raw materials are extracted; finance charges are exacted; an outlet for excess capital is found and so, too, is a large and eager market. But America was a success, while the Third World, which does not fit the Marxian theory, is failing.

The United States was able to withstand the pressures of imperialism, and indeed to profit from them, for a reason that may seem surprising: its wage scales were the highest in the world. This used to be a proud and proper boast. Consequently, if there was any extraction of labor power, it was from Europe, not from America.

It would be making an irrelevant claim to suggest that the relatively high American wages were, except in a few idiosyncratic cases like that of Henry Ford, the result of deliberate policy. High wages were resisted by the entrepreneurs of the time, but they were in fact inevitable, given the small population in relation to the large country. Today's Third World is not so fortunately situated. In general their territories are small and their populations overflowing. There is no way in the foreseeable future for their wage scales to approach the highest in the world. They cannot offer the industrialized world much of a market. They present financiers with opportunities to practice usury rather than investment.

v

Neo-imperialism is as grave a threat to the industrialized world as to the less-developed countries. Before the war, shelves of American five-and-dime stores were plentifully stocked with imported goods—novelties and notions, mostly: figurines from China or Bavaria, costume jewelry from Mexico or India, Christmas-tree ornaments from Czechoslovakia or Japan. Carriage-trade shops made a snobbish point of offering foreign luxuries of all kinds. American industry necessarily imported certain raw materials and in addition specialties such as German optics and Swiss watch movements.

Taken all together, these imports did not amount to much. Even as late as 1950, imports totaled less than $10 billion, or scarcely 3 percent of GNP. Furthermore, the imports generally did not displace existing America industry. In most cases the foreign novelties and specialties were long established, and American competition was not even contemplated.

The situation today is quite different. By 1982, imports were running at a rate of 7.5 percent of GNP, and competition with existing American industry was widespread and intensifying, with no end in sight. Certain industries were particularly hard hit. Electronics and optics were decimated; textiles were cut in half; steel and automobiles were savaged. There was scarcely an industry that did not feel the effects of foreign competition.

Explanations of what was happening were of two sorts. The one most popular with the Chamber of Commerce, the Business Roundtable, and the National Association of Manufacturers was that American wages were too high and American workingmen too concerned about working conditions to be properly productive. Classical economists also shared this view, since they are disposed to prescribe a drop in wages as the cure for most economic ills.

The other explanation was advanced mainly by investment bankers and a few technologically oriented neoclassical economists. According to this view, there is a natural history of business enterprise. When a corporation or—especially—an industry is launched, it grows very rapidly, partly because its initial base is narrow, but mainly because it is vigorous and innovative. As the industry matures, it becomes increasingly preoccupied with consolidating its gains. Too much has been invested in existing factories for newer and more efficient processes to be adopted. As Professor Schumpeter foresaw, the more creative but disorderly entrepreneurial type is replaced by the more reliable but overly cautious manager. Near-term goals are set; attention is directed to next quarter's bottom line rather than toward a glorious future. The path to the executive suite, which had lain open to production and marketing geniuses, now is trod mostly by accountants and lawyers. The enterprise, or the whole industry, stagnates. In Professor Lester Thurow's phrase, it has become a sunset industry and should be written off in favor of some industry whose sun is rising.

vi

Of the two explanations, the wage-scale theory is the more widely accepted. It can even co-opt some liberal arguments in its support, for Galbraith has called attention to the willingness (not so common now as formerly) of big business to raise prices in tacit collaboration with big labor, while Weintraub has emphasized the effect of the unit wage/productivity ratio on inflation.

The wage theory has relied on extensive comparisons of foreign, especially Japanese, industry with American industry. Many of these studies are no doubt casually or deliberately misleading, but there is no need to examine them closely because they are, in any case, inconclusive. There are always two ways of looking at a comparison. In the present instance it may be accepted that American wages are higher than Japanese (though not than Scandinavian, West German, or Swiss). From this fact it may be deduced either that American workers are overpaid—or that Japanese are underpaid. One conclusion is precisely as logical as the other. In view of the history of labor relations, it would seem probable that the latter conclusion is nearer the truth.

This conclusion is all the more certain as one moves from the automobile to the garment industry. The latter is far from a high-wage industry in America, but it is being overwhelmed by Oriental competition. In 1980 in the People's Republic of China, workers in this industry were paid 16 cents an hour; in the Federal Republic of China, the rate was 57 cents an hour; in Hong Kong, it was about a dollar. The rates in Korea and the Philippines were within that range. As a result, imports now account for over half of United States sales of ladies' and children's apparel, up from only 5 percent twenty-five years ago. The sweatshop has reappeared in America, with illegal immigrants held to virtual peonage in conditions approaching those of the Triangle Shirtwaist fire of 1911.

In short, the argument over wages is irrelevant as it is stated. The question is not whether American workers are better paid than foreign workers, but whether American workers are paid a just wage. Not even the most doctrinaire classical economist can seriously propose that American workers be paid only 16 cents an hour; yet if free trade made sense, that is the wage that would be arrived at.

Classical economists are not, of course, primarily concerned about wages or the people who earn them. They contend that cheap imports save consumers so much money that the economy gains enormously from them. This argument is plausible enough so long as each industry is considered separately. If a particular American industry cannot meet Oriental competition, the thing to do might be to scrap it (as Ricardo suggested the Portuguese should give up weaving) and concentrate on something to be sold in the Orient. Displaced workers could be relocated or pensioned off. No one can claim a perpetual right to a special job merely because he or she likes it or is experienced in it.

It is, however, an example of the familiar fallacy of composition to transfer this possibly valid argument about a single industry to the economy as a whole.

And the economy as a whole must be considered, because today there is nothing whatever that cannot be manufactured more cheaply in the Third World than in the developed world. Steel in Brazil, electrical appliances in Singapore, automobiles in Korea, silicon chips in Mexico, textiles everywhere—there is no limit to what can be done. On the basis of the Law of Comparative Advantage, all American industry—hi-tech as well as smokestack—should be shipped abroad, and the United States, the industrial giant of the middle half of the twentieth-century, should return to cultivating its gardens. There is, to be sure, some brave talk about a role in information processing, but with only agriculture and the service industries (including information processing itself) to be informed about, the role at best is not likely to be a large one and at worst would seem to be contemplating one's navel. Since agriculture now employs not quite 3 percent of our labor force (and pays them poorly) and produces 2.8 percent of our GNP, most Americans would have nothing to do and consequently no earnings with which to buy the cheap imports.

Obviously such a scenario is absurd, but there is nothing in classical economics that contradicts it. Just as Keynes showed that a domestic economy does not automatically operate at full employment, it can be said that the world economy does not automatically employ all the available factors of production. In both cases, government intervention is called for.

vii

The absurd conclusion of the classical scenario is duplicated by the sunset/sunrise explanation of international trade. Indeed, the two views differ mainly in their choice of metaphor. The sunset theorists see that once-proud American industries have faltered and been weakened by foreign competition, mainly Oriental. Following their metaphor, they think the phenomenon natural, inevitable, and irreversible. They therefore recommend abandoning such doomed industries to their fate and mobilizing a massive national R & D effort to locate and nurture sunrise industries to take their place. These theorists seem to be no more impressed than was Ricardo by the waste and suffering consequent on the death of an industry. And it seems not to have occurred to them that what happened once can happen again. There is no reason on earth why our new sunrise industries, whatever they may be, cannot be quickly copied in the Third World and subjected to the same low-wage competition as our old industries. Nor is there any reason why our multinationals, having benefited from the national R & D program, should not at once open sunrise factories in the Third World, causing our sun to set before it rises. Investment bankers stand ready to finance them, using our money for the purpose, and relying on our government to bail them out if anything goes wrong.

There are many reasons for regarding the sunrise program with suspicion, not the least of them being the fact that the program's sponsors can foretell the future no better than anyone else. It is not long since they were among the most vocal opponents of the scheme to save Chrysler. To them it was the most obvious of sunset industries, certain to fail eventually; and they proclaimed the attempt to shore it up a most unwise use of public credit, throwing good money after bad.

viii

The Third World will escape from neo-imperialism only as it is able to reduce manufacturing things for the First World and to increase manufacturing things for trading within itself. For many and obvious reasons, this will not be easy, though they will be helped if we help ourselves. That is to say, they will be nudged into trading among themselves if we cut down our labor-extracting trade with them. It is in our interest to protect ourselves from such trade because it hurts our fellow citizens and disrupts our economy. As elsewhere, direct action is called for.

The way to protect is to protect. First we decide that a few of our important industries are threatened *in our home market* by severe competition from foreign industries. Second, we determine whether that threat is made possible by wages or conditions that we would consider exploitative. Third, we refuse entry to goods produced in grossly exploitative conditions.

The proposal is not complicated. It does not cover all industry but only a few industries we declare to be important and threatened in our home market. It does not require elaborate cost accounting (as do the GATT provisions against "dumping") but simply straightforward questions of fact: What are the wage scales? What are the working conditions? Is child labor employed? The proposal does not interfere with foreigners' or multinationals' trade anywhere else in the world. In every respect the proposal is analogous to our present laws refusing entry to contaminated foods or dangerous drugs or unsafe automobiles. Those laws protect Americans as consumers; the proposed law would protect us as workers and, incidentally, as entrepreneurs.

It will be objected that the proposal can't work because it is impossible to compare foreign wage scales and working conditions with ours. How, if the comparisons can't be made, do the critics of the American workingman know he is overpaid? What is proposed is merely the reverse of the critics' coin.

Of course the comparisons can be made, and they will be invidious. The real question is, as the lawyers say, who should have the burden of proof? In the present case, we could reasonably ask those who want access to our markets to prove that their workers are fairly paid and fairly treated by our standards. American unions and American companies would have the right to challenge the proof. No need to make a big fuss about it, any more than a big fuss is now made about determining that certain foreign automobiles don't meet our emissions standards or that certain drugs are inadmissible.

No doubt many will argue against protecting the American standard of living. Two arguments stand out. The first purports to be consumer oriented. Cheap imports, it says, benefit everybody. But they don't benefit those millions whose jobs are taken by the imports, and those other millions who are being forced back to the poverty level.

The second argument purports to be producer oriented. Restrictions on international trade, it says, invite retaliation and threaten all our industries, because exports now represent our margin of profit. To this argument there are three answers: (1) Our really threatened industries—automobiles, steel, textiles, etc.—have already lost their export markets; (2) our biggest export business—agriculture—will probably continue because the world needs it; and (3) we have at home an unexplored market larger than any we might lose.

Our millions of unemployed, plus the millions of working poor, plus their dependents, comprise a "nation" of up to 50 million people—bigger than any but a handful of the 157 members of the UN. In spite of our failures, these people are better educated than the rest of the world, are more familiar with the American work ethic, and are closer to the rest of us in needs and wants. If our national and industrial policies were directed to helping these our fellow citizens so that their undeniable wants became effective economic demands, there would be plenty of domestic business to keep U.S. industry fully occupied and highly profitable.

ix

The skeleton in the protectionist closet is the Smoot-Hawley Tariff, sponsored by reactionary Republicans in 1930 and ever after blamed by junior-high-school civics texts for the Great Depression, the rise of fascism, World War II, the Cold War, and innumerable minor irritations. The analysis doesn't rise even to the level of *post hoc ergo propter hoc*, for the Great Depression was already well under way when Smoot-Hawley was passed, while fascism had been in power in Italy for eight years and was rapidly growing in Germany, and the military was in charge in Japan.

An interesting thing about Smoot-Hawley is that its original impetus came from distress on the farms. Although by the time the bill was passed duties had been raised on almost everything under the sun, the presenting complaint in President Hoover's call for a special session of Congress was largely agricultural. Today there is again distress on the farms, but its cause is different. This time no one is underselling us in our domestic market (except, for some crops, Mexico), or in our international market. The trouble, instead, is that the Poles and others who want our wheat haven't anything to pay us with. The Poles have coal for sale, but so have we—and so do the Germans, the French, the Belgians, the British. (One of the "reindustrializing" schemes that has been advocated involves rebuilding the port of Norfolk to facilitate the export of coal to God knows whom.)

Since the Poles couldn't pay us for our wheat, we had to fall back on our ingenuity. The solution was simplicity itself: We lent them the money. Partly we lent it as a nation through the Export-Import Bank, and partly we had it lent for us by our bankers. Of course, Chase and Citibank and the rest didn't exactly use our money; they used the Arabs' money, deposited with them because of the high interest rates the Federal Reserve Board encouraged, allegedly to fight inflation. Just as bankers become unwitting partners of debtors to whom they lend too much money, we as a nation have become the unwitting partners of the banks that now have shaky foreign loans far in excess of their assets.

The upshot of all this is that we the people of the United States will in effect pay our farmers for the wheat that is in effect given to the Poles. One need have nothing against the Poles to wonder why it is better to give our wheat to them than to poor fellow citizens, whom we expect to feed themselves on a supplement of less than a dollar a day. Charity should no doubt be worldwide, yet it should certainly begin at home.

The result of the banks' loans to Brazil and some others in many ways is worse. The Brazilians invested the money (which wasn't lent to New York City because it was a "bad risk") in building up their industry, particularly steel. Thanks to their low wages, they are now driving American steel out of the world market and to a considerable extent out of the domestic American market. To repay the loans, Brazil has to export still more steel and import less of whatever it imports. This means reducing Brazil's standard of living, and consequently paying its steel workers even less than at present.

If the bankers' scheme succeeds—by no means a certainty—additional American steel workers will lose their jobs. Should the scheme fail, the banks will come crying to Uncle Sam to bail them out (they've already lobbied an increase in our contributions to the International Monetary Fund), and we will in effect have given Brazil the steel mills that are destroying our industry and putting our fellow citizens out of work.

A very high percentage of foreign trade follows the patterns outlined, distorting economies everywhere to the principal benefit of bankers. There are, naturally, many things we want or need to import—oil (because we are too witless to cope with our energy requirements), tungsten, chrome, bauxite, coffee—and there are many things we can, without special government assistance, export to pay for them. But the necessity, or even the desirability, of foreign trade has been grossly oversold.

Trade is one of the modes of civilization. Trade also adds to wealth—the wealth of individuals, of nations, of the world. It does this by increasing and rationalizing employment, for wealth is the product of work. When trade expands employment for both partners, the prosperity of both is advanced, and Ricardo's Law of Comparative Advantage can be said to apply. Conversely, when trade brings about unemployment for one of the partners, its advantage disappears. Trade will always result in some unemployment in a competitive situation, and the unemployment will be compounded where the competition is based on gross wage differentials. If Japanese citizens were to buy up the output of Korea's nascent automobile industry in preference to Subarus and Toyotas, Japanese wealth would be decreased; we may be sure that the Japanese government has imposed effective restrictions.

Microeconomically—that is, company by company—foreign trade can be very attractive. Once a company is successful in its home market—factories built and paid for,
experience gained—it takes little extra effort to open an export business, and economies of scale will make that business extraordinarily profitable at the margin, especially when
stimulated by tax incentives.

When we shift from microeconomics to macroeconomics—
from firm to nation—we find yet again that what is good for
each firm individually is not necessarily good for the nation.
In the circumstances we have been discussing, some (not all)
American exports are being paid for by us in the shape of
high interest rates that inordinately benefit a few, and we
will doubtless bear the further cost of rescuing banks in danger of failing. On the other side, some (not all) American
imports are being paid for by individual citizens in the shape
of their shattered prospects and hopeless poverty.

These outcomes are not divinely ordained. They are the
result of policies deliberately, albeit perhaps blindly,
adopted. Rational policies would be in the direction of that
millennial day when the world standard of living is uniformly
high and trade can be uniformly free.

In the meantime, one would not select extractive or agricultural industries for protection, because in general our
commonwealth will be the stronger the more of our natural
resources remain for future use. For similar reasons, it
would be prudent to be especially attentive to strategic industries: it would be foolish to allow the steel industry to
collapse, regardless of how much cheaper imports might be.
Whatever the market may be, it is not a proper judge of
national interest.

On the other hand, one would look constantly for appropriate ways of removing protective barriers. One would offer
technical assistance to the affected foreign countries (recognizing that in most instances the trouble is caused by our
multinationals), and one would eventually try to make more
promising jobs available to at least some workers in our protected industries. Needless to say, nothing can be done in
the latter direction as long as the economy has millions of

unemployed already searching for such jobs; nor, even if there were true full employment, would vague talk of retraining relieve society of its obligations. If the rest of us have a desperate need to buy cheap sports shirts made in the Orient, the least we can do is make certain that our displaced fellow citizens actually do have decent alternatives.

15

BANKING

What Goes Up Doesn't Necessarily Come Down

i

In the two preceding chapters we have recommended policies that no one can embrace with enthusiasm. Price control and protectionism restrict everyone's activities and expand intrusive bureaucracies that, while not strictly unproductive, in any case produce nothing tangible. The best that can be said for the recommended policies is that they are lesser evils than those they are designed to correct. Price control is a more just way of containing inflation than is the sort of monetary policy recently pursued, and protectionism promises a less traumatic end to neo-imperialism than what currently passes for free trade.

It is conceivable that a more rational corporation law would, by diffusing power more equitably, make it possible for the market to play something approaching its classical role in organizing prices and trade. We can at least wish for such a consummation. It will, nevertheless, be exceedingly difficult to expect anything other than a continuation of lurches on the brink of disaster unless we are able to bring banking under more effective control. Just as war is too important to leave to the generals, money is too important to leave to the bankers.

Money, we will remember from Chapter 5, is not an ordinary commodity like bread, nor are financial services services in the ordinary sense of data processing, motorcycle maintenance, or fast-food purveying. The practical consequences of these theoretical considerations can be quickly shown. If bread is, for whatever reason, overpriced, only the bread bakers languish. We can always eat cake. If, however, money is overpriced—that is, if the interest rate is too high—bankers may prosper rather than repine, for the increase in the rate may offset, or more than offset, a possible fall in the demand for loans. But the rest of the economy will surely languish. We have seen it happen.

That a high interest rate will cause the economy to languish is well understood. For this reason politicians running for reelection anxiously suggest that the Federal Reserve Board do something to bring the rate down. The Federal Reserve Board can undoubtedly do something, probably enough for *ad hoc* political purposes, but it is no longer able, as it once might have been, to play a decisive role in shaping a prosperous economy with full employment. This is because deregulation has turned the banking system into a herd of rogue elephants.

ii

As a function of their size, today's giant corporations have enormous cash flows in both directions. A little experience enables corporate financial officers to operate on a day-to-day basis, estimating fairly closely how much they will take in, and planning quite precisely how much they will need to pay out. Whatever cash they accumulate in excess of these diurnal needs represents wasted opportunity unless they immediately put it out at interest. One week's interest on a million dollars at 12 percent is $2,333, a not inconsiderable sum.

Obviously, this sort of activity, which is at least moderately nerve-racking, is scarcely worth the bother when interest rates are low. It was not extensively practiced in the early postwar years, when the prime rate was 1.50 to 1.75 percent. Corporations then routinely deposited their temporarily unneeded cash in their checking accounts, which drew no interest. Banks liked that, and depended on it.

Gradually, however, interest rates rose. This was largely the doing of the Federal Reserve Board, which was possessed, then as now, of the notion that inflation was an imminent threat (in 1949 the inflation rate was *minus* 1 percent and had reached plus 1 percent a year later). Then as now, the threat was to be exorcised by restricting the money supply. By the end of the 1950s, the prime rate had gone to 4.48 percent; two decades later it was up to 12.67 percent; in December of 1980 it topped out at 21.5 percent. As a result of this surge in rates, there were several tremors in the banking world that went by the name of disintermediation crises. The septusyllabic adjective means that the thrift institutions and to some extent the commercial banks, regulated as they were in the interest rates they could pay, were pushed out of their intermediate position between their biggest depositors and their biggest borrowers, who found ways of getting together more directly to meet their complementary needs. The former big depositors thus got a good bit more for their money, and the former big borrowers had to pay a little bit less for theirs. Then in the late 1970s, the medium-sized depositors rushed to the new money-market mutual funds. The banks suffered, and the thrifts suffered severely.

These crises could obviously have been met in either of two ways. Either the Federal Reserve Board could have relaxed on the money supply, thus sending interest rates back down, or the regulations (most of which had been prompted by the bank failures of the Great Depression) could have been lifted. Needless to say, the bugaboo of inflation and surviving hatred of the New Deal and aversion to regulation and eagerness for high interest rates made the outcome practically inevitable. The negotiable certificate of deposit, introduced in 1960, allowed banks to compete in the money market on the basis of price. In 1970, interest-rate ceilings were suspended for time deposits of more than $100,000; by 1982 the minimum was down to $2,500, allowing banks to compete freely for all but the smallest depositors, whose business was increasingly handled on a fee-for-service basis. In the meantime, NOW accounts allowed banks to pay interest on checking balances, state usury laws were suspended, FDIC insurance was extended, banks were permitted to sell insured money-market funds, there was a general relaxation of restrictions on branch banking, and by 1984 the New Deal reforms were a shambles.

iii

In the summer of 1984, Continental Illinois, the nation's eighth-largest bank, was pulled back from the verge of failure by the action of the FDIC in guaranteeing all its deposits, not merely those under $100,000. Thus a run on the bank was averted. And thus a precedent was set for whenever other banks have trouble. As a practical matter, only the biggest banks are involved, for only they could bring the economy down if they failed. But the impact on deposit insurance is enormous, because 80 percent of the deposits of the biggest banks are currently uninsured, as opposed to only 10 percent in the cases of the others.

Now, if we look back at page 53, we will see that this implicit extension of deposit insurance has changed radically the meaning of M-2, which has now become, in principle, practically indistinguishable from M-1. The various elements of both measures of the money supply are all either legal tender or easily converted into legal tender. And they are now as safe as cash (as a practical matter, safer) because, with lingering doubts about large deposits in small banks, they are explicitly or implicitly insured by the government. Whatever is money should be both liquid and safe, and most of the elements meet these tests.

This is not all. Most of these elements now earn interest, some of course more than others. Hitherto only the elements of M-1A met the above tests for money, for only they were fully liquid and only they were relatively safe. But they did not earn interest. (It is sometimes argued that banks provided depositors, especially large ones, with free services in lieu of interest. It is doubtful that many businesses thought of services as the same as interest, and in any case, most of the services—except for small depositors—still are available in addition to interest.) If you wanted liquidity and safety, you used to have to forgo interest. Now, however, close to 85 percent of M-2 earns interest, and practically all of M-2 is as safe and as liquid as M-1A. And M-2 is more than five times as large as M-1A. These are enormous and fateful changes. At first glance they seem benign, a miraculous case of having our cake and eating it, too. But (adapting a favorite saying of Professor Friedman's) there is no such thing as a free dessert.

For when risk-free money earns high interest the effect on the economy is either inflationary or depressive or not improbably both. The interest that money can earn is a *certain* opportunity cost that businesses must balance against any contemplated enterprise. If the interest on money is 10 percent, no business investment will be made unless it is expected to earn that 10 percent in perfect safety in addition to the cost of borrowing money and, of course, the "normal profit." Thus a given new enterprise will be feasible if the prices of its products can be raised enough to cover that extra 10 percent; otherwise not. When prices are generally raised, that's inflation; when enterprise is generally aborted, that's depression.

iv

Not only does the interest paid on money have a continuous inflationary effect on the price level; it is also a floor below which commercial interest rates cannot fall. Indeed, since it costs banks a point or two or more to do business, the rates they charge tend to be that much higher than the rates they pay. And this floor is maintained by the competition of the banks with each other and with the kinds of businesses (insurance companies, stock brokers, even retail merchandisers) who have been permitted by deregulation to perform banking functions.

Competition is by no means a universal good, and in the case of banking it is almost a universal disaster. Ordinary businesses compete with each other more at the selling end than at the supply end. Their competition at the selling end forces them to exert downward pressure on the prices they pay for their supplies. In the case of banking, the shape of competition is significantly different, because its supply—money—is limited. A bank's first problem is to attract deposits, and the most effective solution is to raise the interest it will pay. Raising the rate is especially important to meet competition from money-market funds and even Treasury bills. A complementary solution is to open branches where depositors (and perhaps borrowers) are. In states that, like Florida, have comparatively few restrictions on branch banking, major intersections are more likely to have four banks than, as formerly, four filling stations. The same search for funds (together with the delights of not even vestigial regulation) encourages the expansion of international banking.

All of this is expensive. Competition forces banks to pay higher and higher interest rates and offer more and more expensive services. As the bankers say, their cost of funds increases; so of course the rates they charge borrowers must increase, too. Deregulation has ripped off the ceiling over interest rates and has put in its place a floor under them—a floor, moreover, that has a tendency to levitate. Because of this levitating floor, the Federal Reserve Board has less and less power to push rates downward (assuming that such an idea ever crossed their minds).

v

Having attracted deposits, the deregulated banks, now thinking of themselves as businesses like any other, are faced with the other half of the ordinary business problem, namely how to sell their expensive product at a profit. Some of the solutions are worth glancing at.

Perhaps the most important, at least in the short run, is the encouragement of speculation, whose deleterious effects we have already discussed. New kinds of speculation are constantly invented. In the mid 1980s, leveraged buyouts absorbed a lot of money at high rates, without in any way increasing production.

Perhaps more important in the long run is the encouragement of agri-business, resulting directly in heart-breaking bankruptcies in the farm belt and indirectly in possibly permanent damage to the ecosystem—a vital subject beyond the scope of this book.

Unquestionably important in its effect on the state of the world is the development of international banking and especially the frantic competition to see who could press the most money on Third World and Communist Bloc nations. As Richard Lombardi has shown, the big banks, bemused by the folk saying that countries don't go bankrupt, have sent vigorous loan officers criss-crossing the world with literally billions of dollars to lend. These loan officers have in effect been salesmen; they have had quotas like salesmen; they have been rewarded on the basis of the amounts of money they have contrived to lend; and they have been known to be careless in investigating the uses to which the money has been put.

In spite of the excited stories that have appeared in the daily press, the trouble with these loans—the trouble from the point of view of the banks, that is—is not that there is scant prospect of their ever being repaid. The trouble is that the interest—generally at rates floating well above domestic rates—cannot be paid. The banks would be perfectly happy to roll the principal over and over, and indeed have done so, if only the interest would keep rolling in forever and ever. If they didn't roll the principal over but somehow collected it, they would have to go to the expense of finding another borrower to press it on.

In all their selling, and especially in the foregoing examples, the banks are forced by competition to concentrate their efforts on those situations in which they can hope to enjoy economies of scale. Once you have an organization capable of handling a corporate takeover, you hunt for more and bigger takeovers to support your organization. Likewise a farmer willing to buy and equip and mortgage thousands of acres is more interesting to you than a lot of people looking for (as a bestseller published in the Depression had it) five acres and independence. And of course it's easier to persuade a possibly rapacious Third World official to build an expensive state-of-the-art sugar refinery than it would be to find and finance several smaller and more practical projects.

vi

Whenever economies of scale are significant, they become a force for concentration. In the modern banking system, this concentration appears not as centralized control but as shared risk. Only a score or so of the largest banks can afford to play a substantial role in international finance, where interest rates are highest, and where the demand for loans is insatiable. The demand was greatly magnified as the world price of oil increased under the management of OPEC. The banks competed to offer the Arabs high interest rates for their winnings, which were then "recycled," also at high rates, in loans to the countries that had been hit hard by the OPEC price increases.

This recycling has made the United States and other major Western countries unwilling partners of the big banks, whose failure cannot be allowed to occur for fear of disrupting all aspects of international trade. But the partnership is broader than that. For the thousands of smaller banks have been lured—or forced by competition—into a more explicit partnership with the big banks. As the cost of funds has increased for all banks, the smaller ones have had to emulate the big ones by making at least some loans at very high interest. This is not merely a search for profits but a struggle for survival. They have managed to survive partly by buying pieces of the foreign loans from the big banks and partly by depositing large sums with the big banks. As a result, the failure of a big bank could bring down not only its commercial depositors but also its small-bank clients, whose larger commercial depositors would in turn be ruined. And the blight would spread. It is for this reason that the threatened failure of Continental Illinois caused so much concern.

Many of those ideologically committed to ending government regulation have been active in devising schemes for private companies to insure large deposits. Yet no one doubts that such insurance would be credible only with the implicit guarantee of the federal government. A private company might, as expected, try to impose rigorous standards on the banks whose deposits it insured, but there would be limits to what it could do. Because of the high cost of funds, a bank could be forced into insolvency by denying it the possibility of making large loans at high interest. The risk in such loans is generally great, but the risk of not making them is immediate. It is probably safe to say that very few loan officers are intentionally sloppy; they are forced to be so by competition. If they aren't sloppy, someone else will be, and they will be out of business. Moreover, it is simply impossible to imagine any insurance company with the necessary resources to guarantee all deposits of any of the big banks. In the end, the federal government would have to stand behind the insurance companies, and we'd be back where we started from—except that the insurance companies would have picked up some fees (and thus further pushed up the banks' cost of funds) for services they could not perform.

vii

When there were elements of risk and illiquidity attached to big deposits, there was a corresponding incentive for prospective depositors to look for ways of investing large sums instead of merely depositing them. That incentive has been removed, and thus the opportunity cost of productive enterprise has been increased. This result seems paradoxical. On the one hand, the failure of the monetary authorities to expand the money supply has been a brake on enterprise. On the other hand, the "monetization" of M-2 has expanded the true money supply more than five times—and this will also put a brake on enterprise.

There is no solution to this paradox short of abandoning the notions that money is a commodity and banking a business like any other. Competition in banking inevitably forces the interest rate up, and it may go higher as the implicit guarantees to the deregulated banks become more explicit. Unless the monetary authorities intervene, there may come a point at which the rogue elephants, no longer able to sell their loans profitably, or to collect on those they have already sold, will choke to death on their expensive deposits. And we all will choke with them.

Short of such a catastrophic point, there is a broad range of points at which, in the ordinary operation of the economy, the interest rate can settle. True to his propensity to psychologize, Keynes first held that the specification of the actual point at any time depends on the psychology of the participants—the animal spirits of entrepreneurs versus the conservatism of bankers. A page or two later, he corrected this view and wrote: "It might be more accurate, perhaps, to say that the rate of interest is a highly conventional, rather than a highly psychological, phenomenon. For its actual value is largely governed by the prevailing view as to what its value is expected to be. *Any* level of interest which is accepted with sufficient conviction as *likely* to be durable *will* be durable."

It cannot be too strongly emphasized that a convention—and especially this convention—is a deliberate creation, a free expression of individual and collective will. It is self-assertion, once more.

Moreover, the conventional rate, whatever it may be, has actual consequences for good or ill. In particular, the rate of interest, because of its influence on the rate of investment, has a powerful effect on the rate of unemployment. High interest results in low investment, which results in high unemployment. And vice versa: in search of a comforting reflection, Keynes observed that "because the convention is not rooted in secure knowledge, it will not always be resistant to a modest measure of persistence and consistency of purpose by the monetary authority." Unfortunately, such persistence and consistency of purpose as the monetary authorities in the United States and the world generally have been able to muster have almost universally been applied in the direction that leads to high unemployment. The rapidly petrifying convention that 6 percent unemployment equals full employment and the ossifying convention that 10 percent is the natural interest rate support each other.

viii

In recent years, the monetary authorities have excused their actions by pointing fingers at the high United States deficit, which will, they claim, result in increased inflation. It is therefore worth stopping a moment to consider the causes for and the effects of the exponential surge of the federal deficit in the 1980s.

According to projections made by the Congressional Budget Office, the tax and spending laws that were in effect on January 1, 1981 (that is, at the end of the Carter administration) would have yielded a *surplus* of $29 billion in 1989. But the laws that were in effect three years later were projected to result in a 1989 deficit of $308 billion.

Projections are in the nature of things imprecise, but the spread here is large enough to indicate a strongly probable trend. The principal causes of this spread were the tremendous increase in military spending, the vast and varied tax cuts of 1981, and the high interest rate.

Military spending is like pyramid building in that there is no end to it. It is also stimulative. In this it is like any government expenditure and indeed any increase in aggregate demand. Businesses produce goods if they foresee a demand for them; so public expenditures, being both large and visible, are especially stimulative. Although we could have wished for a better use of our money, the military build-up was, together with the slight relaxation of monetary controls in the summer of 1982, decisive in the business recovery that started a few months later.

The tax cuts had a different effect. They were intended to stimulate the "supply side," on the theory, whose fallacy we have discussed, that saving leads to investment. Accordingly, the 1981 personal income tax favored the rich, and the corporate tax favored the prosperous, the hope being that those who didn't need money would save it.

This hope was disappointed, and for a simple reason. Since the federal budget was already in deficit, the tax cuts necessarily increased that deficit. The increased deficit had to be funded; that is, bonds to cover it had to be sold. And to whom were they sold? To those who had money, of course, and these were, in general, those who had benefited from the tax cuts. The upshot was that the rich and prosperous were given money with which to buy government bonds. In effect, they were given the bonds, though of course some used their windfall in other ways. The maneuver accomplished as extraordinary a transfer of wealth—and that to people already wealthy—as America has seen.

This was not all. Since the Federal Reserve Board was tightly controlling the money supply, thus keeping the interest rate high, the new bondholders were given a handsome rate of return—13 or 14 percent or more, running thirty years into the future. By 1985, the interest payable on the federal debt was, as Senator Daniel Patrick Moynihan pointed out, approximately equal to the deficit, and the compounding of that interest would more than offset savings that might be made elsewhere in the budget. In consequence, the only way of reducing the deficit, as repeatedly demanded by the Federal Reserve Board, was by raising taxes. That threatened to send the economy into a new depression, because increased taxes mean a reduction in aggregate demand, and a reduction in demand is followed by a depression as surely as an increase in demand is followed by a boom.

This dilemma could have been avoided if the tax cuts had gone to those who would spend them. It could have been avoided if the Treasury and the Federal Reserve Board had cooperated in holding down the interest rate, as they did during World War II. As it happened, however, both fiscal and monetary policies were misdirected.

ix

The way the deficit is said to be bad is in what is called the crowding-out effect. In order to pay its bills, the government must borrow money, and the government will, in the nature of sovereignty, have first call on whatever money is available. As a consequence, private industry must bid against the government for funds, and the law of supply and demand pushes the interest rates up. (The high rates attract foreign—especially oil-related—funds, which in some part finance the deficit. They also keep the dollar "strong," encourage imports and discourage exports, and result in unemployment as well as massive trade deficits—all of which is another story.)

A moment's reflection will show that for the alleged crowding out to have any effect, the money supply must be severely limited, which it is. The severe limitation, however, has nothing to do with the deficit but is imposed by the Federal Reserve Board. The high interest rates, in short, are not the inexorable consequence of impersonal economic laws but rather the intended result of the deliberate policies of the monetary authorities themselves.

The restriction of the United States money supply has been severe. Over the two decades from 1963 to 1983, M-1 in relation to GNP fell 39.3 percent, and M-2 fell 24.4 percent. The severity of the restriction is only suggested by these figures. For the history of those decades was such that a rational monetary authority would have pursued a policy of expansion rather than contraction.

Most important of the reasons for expansion, the labor force increased enormously. First, the postwar baby boom was fully operational by the end of the period, adding millions to the national work force. Second, the anti-discrimination measures of Lyndon Johnson's Great Society, together with a series of Supreme Court decisions responding to suits brought by the NAACP Legal Defense Fund and others, made it possible for millions of blacks to enter the non-agricultural labor force. Third, the modern Women's Movement, launched by Betty Friedan in 1963 with *The Feminine Mystique*, resulted in the self-authorization of the intention of millions of women to escape from what they saw as the stultifying conditions of housewifery. Fourth, the 1970s saw the return to civilian life of close to a million Vietnam veterans and war-industry workers.

There was, of course, some overlapping. It is possible to be a black, a woman, a war veteran, and a member of the baby-boom generation, all at once. Nevertheless, the labor force as a whole increased from 73.8 million men and women in 1963 to 113.2 million in 1983. That is an increase of 39.4 million workers, or 53.3 percent.

Since it has in recent years required a capital investment of about $30,000 to employ one worker in the modern American economy, these additional 39.4 million workers could have been employed only by the investment of the almost unimaginable sum of $1,182,000,000,000—that is, over one trillion dollars. Of course no such investment was made, and the additional workers were not fully employed (although the achievement of the American economy was tremendous in comparison with that of the rest of the world).

Finally, the period we are considering saw the consolidation of a long revolution in the way business is conducted. Until about the time of the New Deal, it was common to see signs in shops reading "In God We Trust. All Others Pay Cash." To be sure, there was a lot of credit available for speculation, but this was available only to the well-to-do, and only they had charge accounts, which they were expected to settle monthly. It was not possible to cash a check except where you were personally known, and not always there. Mortgages were for five years, or often for only one;

they were renewed if your standing remained good, but they were not automatically renewable. Credit was tight, but not much was needed to float the economy.

A second way of doing business lasted from the start of the New Deal to, roughly, the Eisenhower Administration. At the start of the period, Sears-Roebuck and Montgomery Ward shipped only COD or when payment accompanied order, and Macy's still advertised "6% Less for Cash," but these were merely among the last to give in. The FHA and the VA guaranteed mortgages for twenty years at 4 percent, with only 10 percent down (later such mortgages were available for thirty years, with no down payment). Automobiles and washing machines and radios and furniture were sold on the installment plan. In fact, most durable consumers' goods couldn't have been sold otherwise. More people had checking accounts, and almost anyone could cash a check almost anywhere locally. Quite a lot more money was needed to float this economy than had been needed for the previous one, but the government, for various reasons, kept the interest rates low, and the money was made available.

The third way of doing business, characterizing the period we're now in, might be called the credit-card way. Credit cards themselves account for only a small portion of consumer debt (though the portion is larger than the official figures show, since for some reason only bank credit cards are counted as evidence of debt). In any case, almost anyone can buy almost anything almost anywhere on credit. This of course means that the seller has to wait for his money. And the wholesaler then has to wait, and then the manufacturer, and then the producer of raw materials. Where trade a half century ago was largely current, it is now largely afloat. The need for credit—money—is enormous.

In addition, it turns out that this way of doing business is explosively dynamic. Just as the New Deal shift from one-year mortgages at 6 percent (or more) to twenty-year mortgages at 4 percent (or less) resulted in a housing boom, the credit-card shift has brought forth a fantastic expansion in all sorts of consumers' goods, and consequently in the whole economy. In the two decades in question, consumer credit outstanding increased from $81 billion to $467 billion, and mortgage debt went from $278 billion to $1,774 billion.

All these factors—the increase in the labor force, the need for capital investment, and the demand for everyday credit (not to mention the vast but uncharted growth of the underground economy)—should have prompted a rapid expansion of the money supply. If the money supply had merely kept pace with the increase in GNP, M-1 would have reached $858 billion by 1983, instead of the $521 billion it did reach. If it had kept pace with the needs of a fully employed economy, it would probably have had to be at least double what it was.

In sum, the Federal Reserve Board has kept money scarce for twenty years or more. It is because of scarcity that money can earn interest; and the more severe the scarcity, the higher the interest. The Federal Reserve Board and the banking system as a whole—not any Congress nor any President—made the present deficit inevitable and unmanageable. Private enterprise would not have been crowded out of the money markets by high interest rates if the banking system had behaved rationally.

x

While it is generally recognized that a severely limited money supply will support high interest rates or push them higher, it is also widely contended that an increased supply would result in even higher rates. The theory heard on Wall Street is that fear of inflation would bring this about, because it would be anticipated that too much money would be chasing too few goods. We have already discussed this notion of inflation; let us now inquire whether the fear, even if justified, could result in higher rates.

According to the theory, bankers and others with money to lend are unwilling to make loans unless they are reasonably sure of getting not only their money but also their purchasing power back. In inflationary times, the money interest rate that borrowers pay is understood to consist of two parts—the real interest rate and an allowance for inflation. The real interest rate is generally calculated by subtracting the current rate of inflation from the money interest rate. Keynes pointed out that this procedure is faulty because it is the future, not the current, rate of inflation that matters in the case of a loan or any other contract for future performance. However all that may be, it is the notion of a real interest rate that concerns us here, not the way in which it may be calculated.

Assuming that lenders want to get their purchasing power back (with interest), and even that their desire to do so may be contemplated sympathetically, there remains the question of how they are going to manage it when the money supply is expanded. In the Wall Street theory, the lenders foresee inflation and therefore demand a high money rate of interest; and if they don't get it, they don't lend. That is not so easy to do, and not so sensible, either. One is reminded of the unfaithful servant in the Parable of the Talents.

While lenders' strikes regularly plague small and weak countries, and can have partial success even in a country as large and rich as France, it is scarcely possible to imagine one in the United States unless the monetary authorities cooperate (as they did, especially from the fall of 1979 to the summer of 1982, and continued to do, though less firmly, thereafter). Lenders could not bring it off by themselves. One response to an increase in the money supply would no doubt be a shift from long-term to short-term lending, but there would then be enough short-term money around to hold that rate down, and borrowers would happily shift to rolling over short-term loans. Lenders might then try to send their money overseas—a flight from the dollar. Much could be done (given the will to do it) to impede such a flight; but it would not in any case be an unmitigated disaster, since a weaker dollar would reduce imports and stimulate exports and so help close the balance-of-trade gap. Besides, foreign authorities are themselves anxious to reduce interest rates and so can be expected to be cautious about welcoming a flight prompted by falling rates.

The major result of a fall in interest rates (from the point of view of prospective lenders) would be a repeat of the events of the fall and winter of 1982–3: a run-up of the stock and bond markets, because a fall in the interest rate increases the capitalized value of every income-earning asset. When the rate is 10 percent, a security that earns $1 has a capitalized value of $10. If the rate falls to 5 percent, the capitalized value becomes $20.

Prospective lenders who sit on their money during such goings-on will suffer great losses. They may not like the prevailing interest rate, but their choice is between that rate and nothing at all. Convinced though they may be of future inflation, persuaded therefore that the low money interest rate makes the real interest rate even negative, they can do nothing with their money unless they accept the money rate. If, like the unfaithful servant, they bury their money and so preserve it, they will merely forgo all interest, no matter how unreal it seems to them. Inflation or no inflation, the most successful investing (or speculating) strategy is the one that winds up with the most money. That amount of money may have less purchasing power than what one started with, but it certainly has more purchasing power than a smaller amount would have. A negative real interest rate, in apparent contradiction of the laws of mathematics, proves to be greater than zero.

In a confrontation with rational and determined monetary authorities, money can run to speculation, consumption, or investment in productive enterprise; but it can't hide. Speculation can be inhibited by sound taxes and banking regulations, and it often carries its own inhibitions in the shape of high carrying costs and unorganized markets. And no one will object to consumption or productive enterprise, for the lower interest rate will have been managed precisely to increase aggregate demand and stimulate investment.

The money interest rate is what matters to both lenders and borrowers. The so-called real rate, no matter how it may be calculated, does not appear except as a result of the calculation. It is called real, but it has no actual existence. In this it is like the other alleged realities we have encountered: self-interest vs. enlightened self-interest, market value vs. labor value, actual dollars vs. constant dollars, money wages vs. real wages, nominal GNP vs. real GNP. Economists have wasted much time and confused much thought with their propensity to see the world as a dualism, in which, as Charles Peirce said, appearance and reality are like a freight train held together by a feeling of good will between the engineer in the cab and the brakeman in the caboose.

xi

One of Keynes's central ideas was that in a healthy economy prices, including interest rates, are "sticky." A sticky price is not merely slow moving, it is historical, being based on the past and looking forward to the unknowable future. Without such stickiness it is difficult, if not impossible, for businesses to undertake projects that require a long time to bring to fruition, and industry therefore stagnates. This effect can be observed in the contemporary and much deplored concentration of corporate officers' attention on the quarterly or monthly bottom line.

Much of the trouble in the present economy has been due to the fact that interest rates, over the past several decades, have been far from sticky. Their volatility has encouraged speculation and discouraged enterprise. The imposition of stickiness, therefore, should be one of the objectives of reform. Since another of the objectives should be a substantial lowering of interest rates, policy makers are faced with a dilemma. If rates are lowered overnight, the principle of stickiness will be grossly violated, and the economy will be thrown into confusion. But if rates are not lowered overnight, unemployment will continue to be high, and we shall be continuing the injustice of forcing the disadvantaged to pay the cost of the high rates.

Since the thrust of unregulated banking is toward levitation of the rates, little can be done until banking is got under control, and under more comprehensive control than obtained in the past. If that could be done, the monetary authorities could embark on an open policy of bringing the prime rate steadily down to, say, 5 percent over a period of five years, and to 2 or 3 percent after ten years. The time periods are selected because five years is a customary dividing line between short-term and long-term financing, and most bonds issued recently are callable after ten years; consequently comparatively few existing arrangements would be fundamentally upset. This is not to say that no one would be upset. But it is to say that upsets should be considered on their merits, and that the entire economy—especially our ten million or more unemployed fellow citizens—should not be held hostage to protect the privileges and immunities hitherto accorded mere ownership of money.

There are two main weaknesses in the Federal Reserve System: (1) not all forms of banking and quasi-banking are under the system's control, and (2) the system itself is not under political control. The second point will shock those who have not looked at the record. For the record is clear that the experienced bankers and learned experts who have run the Federal Reserve Board during the seventy years of its existence have failed again and again and yet again to understand how business is done and what the banking system should do to make the economy work. In the face of this disastrous record and the awful grief it has caused, not only in the United States but throughout the world, it is absurd to continue to mouth the sanctimonious canard that we can't trust politicians with serious matters. If we can't trust politicians, it is because we don't trust ourselves; and if we don't trust ourselves, it is because we have not understood the meaning of our autonomy.

Only the naïve will fancy that it will be easy to get the banking system under rational control. It can scarcely be expected that today's rogue bankers will go gentle. At the very least, they will make ingenious and determined efforts to find loopholes comparable to those exploited over the last twenty years, and there might even be a surge of high-level loan sharking. Such efforts could be contained if all branches of government—legislative, executive, judicial, and the citizenry—could disabuse themselves of the notion that banking is a business like any other.

Banking policy must be judged not on the prosperity of the bankers, not on the GNP, not even on a low interest rate. A high GNP and a low interest rate are desirable not in themselves but only as contributors to the proper economic objective of free and full employment in a just society.

16

WRAP-UP

A Word or Two Before You Go

i

History is the story of genesis, of how one thing leads to another. It is also, and preeminently, the story of how things go about as far as they can go and of the fresh starts that are then attempted. The fresh starts are revolutions, which may be accompanied by violence but are not necessarily violent. The Copernican, the Newtonian, and the Darwinian revolutions were not violent, but they changed our lives and our ways of looking at our lives. The industrial revolution also did its main work nonviolently, though certainly not without causing suffering.

Revolutions are not inevitable or inexorable. Many are defeated; many more aborted. The truth does not always win, and what appears to be the truth is not always truthful. We could not have become what we are if the Church had been successful in suppressing what Galileo stood for. There was no necessity, before the event, for the Church to fail, hence no necessity for us to become what we are. No Galileo appeared in the Orient or Africa. In the same way, the ideals advanced by the American Revolution might well have been deflected or defeated; their success was not automatic, no matter how well prepared; the colonists could not win without actually winning.

Some revolutions do their work silently, without being noticed even by their leaders, until the work is done. Such was the commercial revolution. Such is the revolution that may now be in progress, marking the end of the modern world. Rejecting absolute space and time, Einstein established the necessity of a particular coordinate system—a particular point of view—in every scientific report and of calculable transformations between systems, thus maintaining a coherent world; yet he could declare, "I do not at all believe in freedom in the philosophical sense." Freud's theory and practice aimed to enable the patient to be in charge of himself; yet Freud, too, was a determinist. Keynes was, above all, the economist of the unknowable future; yet his noneconomic beliefs were heavily influenced by the ahistorical ethics of G. E. Moore. In spite of such personal inconsistencies, these men are all forerunners, if not leaders, in what, for lack of a better name, may be called the self-reflective revolution, whose foundations can be seen in a series of books by Professor John William Miller.

There is no doubt that most current economics is no part of this revolution. On the other hand, there are signs that much current economics is reaching a dead end. It would seem, for example, that not much more can be done with a mathematical analysis of the law of supply and demand than has been done by Professor G. Debreu, whose analysis certainly requires assumptions of a world quite different from our actual world. Though the prestige of this kind of thinking remains high enough for it to be awarded the Nobel Memorial Prize, critics are beginning to wonder why it has not yet succeeded even on its own unrealistic terms.

Much economic discussion proceeds as though production and consumption had a life of their own; but it is the producers and consumers who are alive. No one knows what or how much a more just economy would produce. But this will not be the first question in any reflective person's mind, for the maintenance of a just society of civilized men and women would be production enough.

ii

We have come a long way pretty fast and may therefore profit from a backward glance o'er travel'd roads. We started with the commonplace observation that contemporary schools of economics are in disarray. Inquiring why this should be, we concluded that their almost universal grounding in half-digested psychology, especially when coupled with procedures borrowed from classical physics, has made it impossible for them to define rational objectives. Rationality implied autonomy, whose conditions we tried to suggest, and which became our touchstone thereafter.

Now at the end, let me stand in the first person singular and say with the most solemn emphasis that I believe that the analyses of the middle chapters and the tentative proposals of the concluding chapters have, and can have, no other ground than the rational autonomy of men and women. If this book has a single most important point, it is that economics is not a natural science or analogous to a natural science, but a branch of ethics. I am well aware that many people—perhaps most—are irritated by philosophical talk (much of which also irritates me) and are inclined to choose among analyses and programs those that most appeal to them directly. I shall certainly not be distressed if I have managed to appeal to such people.

Nevertheless, I hold that the shape of this story of economics is as important as its details, and I therefore offer a quick outline of the main points: Because rationality is dynamic, money, the essential economic concept, is dynamic in all respects—as a measure of value, as a store of value, and as a medium of exchange. It is for this reason, and only for this reason, that attempts to establish an absolute standard do not "work." Because one can be oneself only in society, exchange is necessary to autonomy, and economic exchange is acceptable only if it fosters the autonomy of all partners to it. Because autonomy is dynamic, it is expressed in what people do, and economic doings involve production and consumption. Because the economy is dynamic, production and consumption are defined by structure; so producers' goods and consumers' goods are distinguished not by their qualities but by their functioning. Because whatever is dynamic is incomplete, the future is unknown and unknowable, making it important to distinguish carefully among gambling, speculating, and investing in production. Because production requires capital, and capital itself is a product of labor, capital cannot be more virtuous than labor. From this proposition, and from a special definition of profit, there follows the Labor Theory of Right.

And it is on a Labor Theory of Right that the chapters ensuing are based. These chapters, advocating policy after policy contrary to the recommendations of conventional economics, can, I am persuaded, carry conviction only if the analyses of the opening chapters are accepted. Conventional economics is a mighty structure. We do it wrong, being so majestical, to offer it the show of violence. It is a historical force that has changed the world immeasurably for the better and will itself change as we are ready to understand the reasons for its failures. At the very least, understanding should give us the assurance to oppose policies that would compound the failures.

Whatever is done will be our doing.

INDEX

housing, 105–106, 141
Hull, Cordell, 169
human beings, fallibility of, 39
Hume, David, 43, 162
Huxley, Thomas Henry, 23
hyperinflation, 56–57

imperialism, 171–174
 capitalism and, 171
 gunboat, 171–172
 labor extraction in, 173–174
 Marxian theory of, 171, 173, 175
 multinational corporations and,
  172–173
 neo-, 171–174, 175
income, personal:
 distribution of, 164–166
 U.S. total, 164
income taxes, see taxes
India, Japan vs., 95
indices, 1–2, 58–60
 food, 58–59
 as harmful, 60
 industrial price, 59
 market baskets and, 58–59
 price level, 55
 reliability of, 98–99
industry:
 entrepreneurs and, 81
 extractive, 185
 garment, 177–178
industry, U.S.:
 Asian industry vs., 177, 178, 179
 competition in, 175–176
 imports and exports in, 181–182,
  184–185
 before World War II, 175–176
inflation, 59–60, 153–167
 classical view of, 161–162
 cost-push, 162, 164
 explanations for, 161–164
 fixed incomes and, 159–161
 full employment and, 158
 income distribution and, 164–166
 interest rates and, 120, 161
 measures against, 159–160
 modern, 162
 price control and, 163–164
 prices vs. wages in, 163

price-value relationship and, 70
 as recurrent problem, 2
 in Weimar Republic, 56–57
interest:
 compound, 103–104
 profit vs., 110
 on risk-free money, 190–191
interest rates, 119–120, 188–190, 199
 competition in banking and, 192, 196
 inflation and, 120, 161
 investment, unemployment and,
  196–197
 money supply and, 202–205
 speculation and, 118–120
 sticky prices and, 205
 surges in, 189
interests, 16
 economic vs. noneconomic, 73–74
 self-, see self-interest
international banking, 193–195
international trade, 169, 181–182,
  184–185
 removal of barriers in, 185–186
 sunrise/sunset explanation of,
  179–180
inventory, 29–30
inverse-square law, 23, 30
investments:
 capital, 105–106
 interest rates, unemployment and,
  196–197
 new, 116–117
 old vs. new, 116
investors, functionless, 161
invisible hand, 6
 competition and, 138
 labor and, 89
 price and, 71, 75, 135
 public policy and, 153
 sovereignty and, 7
Iron Law of Wages, 134
Isherwood, Baron, 100, 101

James, William, 72–73
Japan, 95, 147–148, 177
Jefferson, Thomas, 128
Jevons, William Stanley, 24–26, 28, 30
Johns Manville, 124, 141–142
Johnson, Lyndon B., 200

About the Author

George P. Brockway was born in Portland, Maine. He is a graduate of Williams College (which gave him an honorary Litt. D. in 1982) and did graduate work at Yale before entering on a career as a book publisher. He was for many years editor and CEO of W. W. Norton & Company (which is, incidentally, employee-owned) and is president of the board of governors of Yale University Press. His first writing in the general field of economics was the chapter "Business Management" in *What Happens in Book Publishing*, edited by Chandler Grannis. He writes a monthly column on economics for *The New Leader* under the rubric "The Dismal Science" and has contributed articles to the *Journal of Post Keynesian Economics* and other magazines. He has published a brief monograph entitled *Political Deals That Saved Andrew Johnson* (he is an honorary fellow of the Society of American Historians) and is coauthor with his wife, Lucile H. Brockway, an anthropologist, of a travel book on Greece. They are the parents of seven children and live in Chappaqua, New York.